MW00939822

LARRY J MEYER

Rhine River Cruise Travel Guide 2024

The Essential Guide to Planning the Perfect Rhine River Cruise: Uncover Hidden Gems, Cultural Delights, and Luxurious Adventures Along Europe's Majestic Waterway

Copyright © 2023 by LARRY J MEYER

All rights reserved. No part of this publication may be reproduced, stored or transmitted in any form or by any means, electronic, mechanical, photocopying, recording, scanning, or otherwise without written permission from the publisher. It is illegal to copy this book, post it to a website, or distribute it by any other means without permission.

First edition

This book was professionally typeset on Reedsy.
Find out more at reedsy.com

Contents

Chapter 1: Introduction

Welcome aboard the timeless currents of the Rhine River, a venerable waterway weaving through the heart of Europe, beckoning travelers to discover its storied past, vibrant present, and boundless allure. As you prepare to embark on a journey that melds history with modernity, culture with breathtaking landscapes, allow this comprehensive guide to illuminate your path and enrich your Rhine River cruise experience in 2024.

Spanning over a thousand kilometers, the Rhine River stands as a testament to Europe's rich tapestry of heritage and natural beauty. From the picturesque shores of Switzerland, meandering through the lush valleys of Germany, and embracing the Netherlands' bustling ports, each bend in its serpentine course unveils a new chapter in this timeless saga.

This guide is meticulously curated to serve as your compass, offering an array of insights, tips, and recommendations to navigate this remarkable voyage seamlessly. Whether you're an intrepid explorer seeking the river's hidden gems or a connoisseur of culture eager to savor the region's finest offerings, this guide aims to cater to every traveler's aspiration.

Prepare to be enchanted by the Rhine's iconic landmarks. From the breathtaking Rhine Falls in Schaffhausen to the enchanting medieval charm of towns like Strasbourg and Cologne, every stop along this illustrious waterway boasts its own unique blend of history and allure. Discover the awe-inspiring majesty of castles perched atop hillsides and vineyards painting the landscape with verdant hues, each telling a tale of centuries past.

As you delve deeper into this guide, anticipate a wealth of practical advice designed to optimize your journey. From packing essentials tailored to varying seasons to insider tips on securing the best vantage points for capturing those unforgettable moments, we've left no stone unturned in our quest to enhance your comfort and enjoyment.

Indulge in the gastronomic delights that dot the riverbanks, sampling the delectable array of local cuisines and world-class wines that characterize each region. From the hearty flavors of German schnitzels to the delicate pastries of French patisseries, allow your taste buds to embark on their own unforgettable expedition.

Moreover, immerse yourself in the vibrant tapestry of local cultures and traditions that thrive in the Rhine's charming towns and cities. Engage with locals, explore bustling markets, and revel in the arts, music, and festivities that breathe life into these historic locales.

While this guide serves as an invaluable resource, we also encourage you to embrace spontaneity and serendipity along your journey. Allow yourself to wander through cobblestone streets, stumble upon hidden gems, and create your own narratives that will forever intertwine with the Rhine's storied legacy.

As you embark on this adventure along the Rhine River in 2024, let this guide be your trusted companion, illuminating the path to unforgettable experiences and lifelong memories. Prepare to be captivated by the river's timeless beauty and the myriad wonders that await at each port of call. Bon voyage!

Overview of Rhine River Cruises

The Rhine River Cruise! Prepare to embark on a journey where history whispers from vine-cloaked hills, fairytale castles pierce the horizon, and charming towns nestle like jewels along the water's edge. This is not merely a cruise; it's a tapestry woven with ancient legends, cultural mosaics, and landscapes that ignite the soul.

Whispers of the Past: The Rhine, Europe's lifeblood, has borne witness to millennia of human drama. Romans marched on its banks, medieval knights guarded its fortresses, and the whispers of Romantic poets still echo in its valleys. Each bend reveals a chapter in history, from the grandeur of Cologne Cathedral to the haunting ruins of the Rheinfels Castle. As you glide past these sentinels of time, imagine the whispers of emperors and troubadours carried on the breeze, painting your journey with the magic of bygone eras.

A Tapestry of Landscapes: The Rhine is a master storyteller, each stretch revealing a different facet of its captivating personality. In the Upper Middle Rhine Valley, designated a UNESCO World Heritage Site, dramatic cliffs adorned with castles rise majestically from the river's embrace. Further south, verdant vineyards unfurl like emerald carpets, punctuated by quaint villages and bustling cities. As you approach the Netherlands, the river widens, transforming into a serene waterway flanked by windmills and charming Dutch towns. Each vista is a postcard come to life, inviting you to step ashore and delve deeper into its allure.

A Symphony of Cultures: The Rhine is a river of contrasts, where ancient traditions dance with modern vibrancy. Stroll through the cobbled streets of Strasbourg, France, and marvel at the Gothic splendor of its cathedral. In Cologne, Germany, witness the awe-inspiring Cologne Cathedral, a master-piece of medieval architecture. Sample the world-renowned Riesling wines of the Rheingau region, or lose yourself in the festive spirit of Oktoberfest in Munich. Each town along the way unfolds a unique cultural tapestry, waiting to be savored and embraced.

Beyond the Surface: A Rhine River Cruise is more than just sightseeing; it's an immersion into the very essence of Europe. Bike along the riverbanks, soaking in the fresh air and breathtaking panoramas. Participate in wine tastings in centuries-old cellars, savoring the fruits of the sun-drenched vineyards. Hike through ancient forests, unearthing hidden ruins and whispering waterfalls. Every moment is an opportunity to connect with the land, the people, and the spirit of the Rhine.

Quick Facts for the Savvy Voyager:

- **Time Zone:** Central European Time (CET)
- **Currency:** Euro (€)
- **Languages:** German, French, Dutch, English spoken widely
- **Seasonality:** Spring (April-May) and autumn (September-October) offer ideal weather and smaller crowds. Summer (June-August) is bustling and warm, while winter brings a wonderland of festive markets and cozy charm.
- **Cruise Lines:** Viking, Avalon Waterways, AmaWaterways, Emerald River Cruises, and Scenic River Cruises are among the many reputable lines offering Rhine River cruises.

Embarking on a Rhine River Cruise is not just a vacation; it's an escape into a world where history, culture, and breathtaking landscapes intertwine. So, pack your sense of wonder, lace up your walking shoes, and prepare to be enchanted by the magic of the Rhine.

Remember, this is just a starting point. Feel free to delve deeper into specific destinations, cultural experiences, or historical aspects that pique your interest. The Rhine River Cruise is a journey tailor-made for your own exploration and discovery.

Why Choose a Rhine River Cruise in 2024

Forget the crowded airports and jostling for sun loungers. Picture yourself gliding serenely along the Rhine River, the sun dappling ancient castles clinging to emerald cliffs, quaint villages nestled in vine-laced valleys, and the aroma of freshly baked pretzels wafting from cobbled streets. This, my friends, is the magic of a Rhine River Cruise – a journey woven from history, romance, and breathtaking beauty. And if you're considering a European getaway in 2024, here are 7 compelling reasons why the Rhine should be your captain's call:

1. Unpack Once, Unwind Endlessly: Imagine the bliss of ditching the daily repacking ritual. On a Rhine River Cruise, your luxurious cabin becomes your floating haven, gliding effortlessly from one charming town to the next. No more late-night train dashes or frantic airport check-ins; simply rise, savor a gourmet breakfast, and step out onto your private balcony to watch the world unfold at your own pace.

2. A Fairytale Corridor: The Rhine has whispered tales for centuries, and its banks are studded with the whispers of history. Majestic castles, like the legendary Lorelei, loom dramatically, their towers echoing with tales of chivalry and intrigue. Quaint medieval towns, like Rüdesheim with its cobbled lanes and half-timbered houses, transport you to a bygone era, while vibrant metropolises like Cologne offer a taste of modern-day vibrancy. Every bend unveils a new chapter, each stops a brushstroke on the canvas of your unforgettable journey.

3. A Culinary Carnival: Forget generic buffets and lukewarm room service. Rhine River cruises elevate your palate to new heights. Savor regional delicacies paired with perfectly matched wines, all prepared by skilled chefs using the freshest local ingredients. Imagine indulging in melt-in-your-mouth Black Forest cake in Freiburg, sampling crisp Riesling in the Mosel Valley, or savoring hearty sausages washed down with local Kölsch beer in

Cologne. Each meal is an adventure for the senses, a celebration of the region's rich culinary tapestry.

4. Immerse Yourself, effortlessly: No need to be a seasoned explorer to delve into the heart of Europe. Rhine River cruises offer a seamless blend of guided excursions and independent exploration. Disembark in charming towns, join walking tours led by local experts, or simply wander at your own pace, soaking in the atmosphere. From visiting UNESCO World Heritage sites like the Rhine Gorge to exploring vibrant Christmas markets in December, every day is an opportunity to discover something new and unique.

5. A Toast to Tranquility: Picture yourself lounging on a sun deck, a glass of Riesling in hand, as the world glides by. The gentle rhythm of the river, the verdant tapestry of vineyards, and the quaint villages dotting the banks create a symphony of serenity. Whether you seek solace in a spa treatment or lose yourself in a captivating novel on your balcony, the Rhine River offers an escape from the everyday, a chance to reestablish a connection with nature and oneself.

6. A Celebration of Christmas Spirit: If you yearn for a magical Christmas experience, then a Rhine River cruise in December is a dream come true. Picture twinkling lights adorning charming towns, festive markets overflowing with handcrafted ornaments and delectable treats, and the scent of mulled wine warming the air. Christmas carols fill the crisp air as you explore enchanting towns like Rüdesheim or Cochem, their festive spirit seeping into your soul. It's a Christmas experience you'll cherish forever.

7. Beyond the River: The Rhine is a gateway to Europe's heart. From vibrant Amsterdam to the majestic Swiss Alps, many cruises offer exciting extensions to complement your river journey. Explore the canals and museums of Amsterdam, hike through the breathtaking landscapes of Switzerland, or delve into the cultural treasures of Vienna. These add-ons seamlessly blend with your cruise, creating a truly comprehensive European adventure.

So, ditch the ordinary and embrace the extraordinary. In 2024, let the Rhine River be your chariot, whisking you away on a journey of history, romance, and unparalleled beauty. With every bend in the river, discover a new reason to fall in love with Europe, and maybe even yourself.

Chapter 2: Planning Your Rhine River Cruise

With careful planning, you can go on an exciting Rhine River Cruise. Discover the best times to sail, choose the greatest cruise line and type, and methodically arrange your itinerary. Navigate budgetary considerations with cost-effective recommendations, providing a flawless and delightful experience as you explore the historic Rhine's picturesque wonders.

Best Time to Cruise the Rhine

Determining the best time for a Rhine River cruise is important for an unforgettable journey. Enjoy the bright hues of spring with blossoming landscapes or the comforting ambiance of fall foliage. Choose your optimum season for nice weather and fewer crowds, assuring an immersive and wonderful Rhine cruise experience.

For the Wine Enthusiast:

- **Harvest Season (September-October):** Immerse yourself in the intoxicating swirl of the Rhine's viticulture. Sip sun-kissed Riesling beneath the golden canopy of the Mosel Valley, celebrating in vibrant wine festivals. Learn the secrets of centuries-old vineyards, your senses tickled by the aroma of fermenting grapes and the clinking of glasses. Dine with local winemakers in charming villages, tasting the terroir of the land in every sip.

- **Spring Blossoming (April-May):** Witness the rebirth of the vineyards, the air sweet with the promise of future vintages. Hike through emerald hills dotted with delicate Riesling blooms, and learn the delicate art of pruning at historic wineries. Savor the first fruits of the season – crisp white asparagus and juicy strawberries – paired with refreshing springtime Rieslings. Explore hidden wine cellars along the Middle Rhine, a treasure trove of vintage gems waiting to be discovered.

For the History Seeker:

- **Roman Echoes (March-May):** Walk in the footsteps of emperors, where Roman legions marched and ancient cities thrived. Explore the Saalburg Roman Fort, its walls whispering tales of battles and glory. Stand atop the mighty Rheinfels Castle, a sentinel guarding the Rhine for centuries. Delve into the medieval mystique of Rüdesheim, its cobbled streets echoing with the footsteps of troubadours and knights.
- **Autumnal Tapestry (September-November):** Witness the Rhine Valley's past painted in fiery hues. Hike through the ruins of Rheinfels Castle, imagining the lives that once unfolded within its moss-covered walls. Explore the Heidelberg Castle, a testament to Renaissance grandeur, its sandstone glowing under the autumn sun. Discover hidden Roman remains nestled among vineyards, remnants of a forgotten era whispering beneath the changing leaves.

For the Adventure Aficionado:

- **Summer Sun (June-August):** Embrace the Rhine's sun-drenched energy. Glide through rapids on a thrilling whitewater rafting adventure, the cool spray invigorating your senses. Scale the rugged cliffs of the Lorelei Rock, the wind whipping through your hair as you conquer the legend. Cycle along the riverbank, a blur of emerald hills and charming villages rushing past. Challenge yourself on challenging hikes through the Black Forest, rewarded with breathtaking panoramas and hidden waterfalls.

- **Spring Awakening (April-May):** Witness the Rhine reawaken from its winter slumber. Kayak through the mist-shrouded valleys of the Taunus Mountains, the crisp air invigorating your spirit. Embark on adrenaline-pumping mountain bike trails, weaving through ancient forests and hidden ruins. Rent a paddleboat and conquer the gentle rapids of the Rhine, feeling the sun warm your skin and the water lap against your oars.

For the Soul Searcher:

- **Winter's Enchantment (December-February):** Glide through a fairytale wonderland, snow-dusted castles mirrored in the glassy river. Find solace in the quietude of ancient forests, the snow muffling the world into a serene hush. Cozy up by crackling fireplaces in charming cafes, a steaming mug of hot chocolate warming your hands as you watch the snowflakes dance. Seek the magic of candlelit Christmas markets, their twinkling lights and festive music igniting a sense of wonder.
- **Spring's Renewal (April-May):** Witness the Rhine's rebirth, a symphony of new life unfolding before your eyes. Hike through meadows carpeted with wildflowers, the air buzzing with the joy of returning birds. Take a yoga class on a sun-drenched deck, the gentle lapping of the water harmonizing with your breath. Discover hidden meditation spots amidst ancient ruins, the whispers of the past mingling with the peace of the present.

For the Romantic:

- **Winter (December-February):** Glide through a winter wonderland, with snow-dusted castles and twinkling Christmas markets lining the banks. Cozy up by crackling fireplaces in historic hotels, sipping hot chocolate and watching the snow fall. Embark on a horse-drawn carriage ride through a fairytale village, wrapped in the warmth of a woolen blanket. Experience the magic of candlelit Christmas Eve services in a medieval cathedral, and soak in the enchanting atmosphere.

- **Summer (June-August):** Enjoy the lazy charm of summer evenings on the Rhine. Sip cocktails on a sundeck as the sun dips below the horizon, painting the sky in fiery hues. Rent a private boat and explore hidden coves, the gentle rhythm of the water lulling you into tranquility. Dance the night away at a riverside festival under the starlit sky, feeling the vibrant energy of the Rhine Valley.

For the Foodie:

- **Autumn (September-November):** Indulge in the bounty of the harvest season. Savor the sweet grapes of the Mosel Valley, celebrating in vibrant wine festivals. Sample hearty stews and local cheeses in cozy taverns along the Middle Rhine, warmed by the crackling fire. Learn the art of gingerbread baking in a charming Christmas market, and fill your senses with the aroma of mulled wine and roasted chestnuts.
- **Spring (April-May):** Discover the freshest flavors of the Rhine Valley. Wander through bustling farmers' markets, overflowing with asparagus, strawberries, and the first tender greens. Sample local specialties like "Handkäs" cheese and "Spundekäs" in quaint villages. Enjoy a picnic on a sun-drenched vineyard, surrounded by the scent of blooming grapevines and the clinking of glasses.

So, dear traveler, let your heart be your compass. Whether you crave epicurean delights, historical whispers, romantic serenades, adventurous thrills, or serene sanctuaries, the Rhine River will orchestrate a symphony of experiences tailored to your soul. Choose your season, raise the anchor, and let the River Rhapsody begin!

Choosing the Right Cruise

Choosing the best Rhine River cruise enhances your journey. Discover various kinds of cruises and themes, ranging from luxury vessels to themed excursions. Explore popular cruise lines, each with its own set of amenities and itineraries.

Find the perfect match to ensure a delightful journey along the historic and scenic Rhine.

Cruise Types and Themes

Rhine River cruises aren't one-size-fits-all experiences. Each voyage is meticulously crafted around a specific theme, ensuring a journey that resonates with your soul. Consider these alluring possibilities:

1. **Classic Rhine**: These timeless itinerary traces the river's most iconic stretch, from Cologne's magnificent cathedral to the Lorelei's legendary rock, with stops at fairytale castles like Marksburg and charming towns like Rüdesheim. Lines like Viking, Avalon Waterways, and Emerald Cruises excel in this realm, offering elegant ships, insightful excursions, and impeccable service.

2. **Christmas Markets:** Imagine strolling through twinkling Christmas markets, the air scented with mulled wine and gingerbread, as you glide past snow-dusted landscapes. Tauck and Scenic Cruises master this festive wonderland, weaving fairytale villages with bustling markets, nativity scenes, and heartwarming traditions into their itineraries.

3. **Wine & Gastronomy:** For gourmands, Rhine River cruises offer a tantalizing adventure through renowned wine regions, from the Rheingau's Riesling to the Mosel's Pinot Noir. Uniworld and A-Rosa River Cruises curate voyages that pair exquisite onboard dining with winery tours, gourmet tastings, and Michelin-starred dinners, turning every meal into an epicurean journey.

4. **Active & Adventure:** Not all river cruises are about leisurely sipping coffee on the sundeck. Some lines, like AdventureSmith Explorations and APT Touring, cater to the adventurous spirit, offering exhilarating hikes through the Black Forest, bike rides along scenic vineyards, and kayaking excursions on the Rhine's tributaries.

Popular Cruise Lines

With so many excellent lines plying the Rhine's waters, choosing one can feel like deciphering an ancient map. But fear not, for here's a glimpse into some of the leading players:

Viking River Cruises: Renowned for their sleek Scandinavian design, spacious cabins, and cultural enrichment programs, Viking offers an upscale and immersive experience.

- **Website:** https://www.vikingcruises.com/
- **Address:** 19310 Fallbrook Avenue, Suite 100, Chatsworth, CA 91311
- **Fees:** Variable based on itinerary and season
- **Amenities:** Infinity pool, spa, onboard entertainment, included excursions

Avalon Waterways: Known for their innovative "active & discovery" philosophy, Avalon features modern ships with panoramic views, bicycles for independent exploration, and engaging shore excursions.

- **Website:** https://www.avalonwaterways.com/
- **Address:** 1371 Catalina Drive, Suite 200, Ontario, CA 91761
- **Fees:** Variable based on itinerary and season
- **Amenities:** Open-air Sky Deck, fitness center, complimentary bicycles, cultural lectures

Emerald Cruises: Embracing a casually elegant atmosphere, Emerald boasts contemporary ships with spacious balconies, all-inclusive dining, and friendly service.

- **Website:** https://www.emeraldcruises.com/river-cruises
- **Address:** 635 Park Avenue, Suite 1001, New York, NY 10065
- **Fees:** Variable based on itinerary and season

- **Amenities:** Panorama Restaurant, wellness center, complimentary Wi-Fi, self-service laundry

Scenic Cruises: Offering luxurious "Space Ships" with private balconies and innovative dining experiences, Scenic caters to travelers seeking a touch of indulgence.

- **Website:** https://www.scenicusa.com/group-travel
- **Address:** 8258 NW 17th Avenue, Miami, FL 33147
- **Fees:** Variable based on itinerary and season
- **Amenities:** Butler service, in-suite dining, private balconies, complimentary laundry

Tauck: Renowned for their exceptional land tours integrated into cruises, Tauck offers an in-depth cultural experience with expert guides and immersive shore excursions.

- **Website:** https://www.tauck.com/
- **Address:** 45-47 Main Street, PO Box 50, New Canaan, CT 06840
- **Fees:** Variable based on itinerary and season
- **Amenities:** Included guided tours, expert lecturers, cultural entertainment

A-Rosa River Cruises: Known for their sleek, contemporary ships and focus on wellness, A-Rosa offers a relaxed and rejuvenating experience. Imagine yourself practicing yoga on the sundeck as the morning mist swirls over the river, then indulging in a spa treatment with locally sourced ingredients.

- **Website:** https://www.arosa-cruises.com/: https://www.arosa-cruises.com/
- **Address:** 30, rue du Grand Duc Jean, L-1445 Luxembourg
- **Fees:** Variable based on itinerary and season
- **Amenities:** Spa with sauna, steam room, and massage treatments, fitness

center, yoga classes, indoor and outdoor pools

Uniworld: Renowned for their innovative experiences and focus on local culture, Uniworld offers themed cruises that delve deeper into specific regions and interests. Imagine yourself joining a winemaking workshop in the Mosel Valley, learning the secrets of traditional Riesling production, then savoring the fruits of your labor during a candlelit dinner in a centuries-old wine cellar.

- **Website:** https://www.uniworld.com/: https://www.uniworld.com/
- **Address:** 1500 Coral Way, Suite 200, Miami, FL 33134
- **Fees:** Variable based on itinerary and season
- **Amenities:** Themed excursions, cultural enrichment programs, onboard cooking classes, expert lecturers

AdventureSmith Explorations: For the truly adventurous, AdventureSmith Explorations offers active itineraries focused on hiking, biking, and kayaking through the Rhine Valley. Imagine yourself conquering challenging trails through the Black Forest, your heart pounding with exhilaration as you reach breathtaking viewpoints.

- **Website:** https://www.adventuresmithexplorations.com/: https://www.adventuresmithexplorations.com/
- **Address:** 625 S. Market Street, Suite 800, Seattle, WA 98104
- **Fees:** Variable based on itinerary and season
- **Amenities:** Guided hikes and bike tours, kayaking excursions, outdoor gear rentals, expert naturalists

APT Touring: Similar to AdventureSmith, APT Touring offers active itineraries with a focus on cultural immersion. Imagine yourself learning traditional cheesemaking in a Swiss village, then cycling through rolling vineyards in Alsace, France.

- **Website:** https://www.aptouring.com/: https://www.aptouring.com/

- **Address:** 400 George Street, Suite 1800, Sydney, NSW 2000, Australia
- **Fees:** Variable based on itinerary and season
- **Amenities:** Guided hikes and bike tours, cultural immersion experiences, local cooking classes, expert historians

Remember, the journey begins before you set sail. Consider your budget, travel style, and desired level of activity when choosing your perfect Rhine River voyage.

Do you crave leisurely days soaking in the scenery from the sundeck, or do you yearn for active exploration through cycling, hiking, and kayaking? Here's how to match your energy level to the ideal cruise:

- **Low-Key Leisure:** Lines like Avalon Waterways and Emerald Cruises offer spacious ships with comfortable sundecks, onboard entertainment, and included walking tours in charming towns. You can spend your days leisurely sipping coffee, admiring the scenery, and indulging in spa treatments. Evenings will likely involve onboard entertainment, fine dining, and perhaps a stroll through a riverside town.
- **Moderate Exploration:** Viking River Cruises and A-Rosa River Cruises strike a balance between relaxation and activity. They offer a mix of guided excursions, like visits to castles and museums, with free time to explore towns independently. You can choose to walk, bike, or join optional excursions for hiking or kayaking. Evenings offer onboard entertainment, cultural lectures, and a variety of dining options.
- **High-Octane Adventure:** If you crave an active adventure, lines like AdventureSmith Explorations and APT Touring are your ideal match. They offer itineraries packed with hiking through the Black Forest, challenging bike rides along scenic vineyards, and kayaking excursions on the Rhine's tributaries. Some cruises even include rock climbing, spelunking, and whitewater rafting for the ultimate adrenaline rush. Expect evenings to be spent sharing stories of your exploits over campfire dinners or enjoying local taverns.

Itinerary Planning

Crafting your Rhine River itinerary unlocks a tapestry of captivating experiences. Explore medieval castles, vineyard-draped hills, and charming towns along this historic waterway. Tailor your journey, balancing cultural excursions and scenic delights, ensuring an enriching and personalized exploration of the Rhine's timeless beauty.

The Grand Panorama (Estimated Price: $3,500 - $5,000)

For those seeking a comprehensive Rhine experience, the classic Amsterdam-to-Basel itinerary is a timeless choice. In Amsterdam, marvel at the gabled houses and canals before embarking on a leisurely bike ride through Dutch countryside. In Cologne, ascend the mighty cathedral and savor a local Kölsch beer in the charming Altstadt. In Rüdesheim, sip Riesling in a fairytale-like tavern overlooking the legendary Lorelei rock. In Heidelberg, climb the hill to the majestic castle and marvel at the panoramic views. This itinerary offers a perfect blend of history, culture, and scenic beauty, ideal for first-time cruisers seeking a taste of everything.

Website: https://www.vikingrivercruises.com/cruise-destinations/europe/rhine-getaway/2023-amsterdam-basel/index.html

For the History Buff (Estimated Price: $2,500 - $3,500)

If the echoes of the past resonate within you, delve deeper into the Rhine's rich tapestry. In Mainz, explore the Gutenberg Museum, birthplace of the printing press, and trace the footsteps of Roman emperors. In Koblenz, ascend the Ehrenbreitstein Fortress, a sentinel overlooking the confluence of the Rhine and Mosel rivers. In Cochem, step back in time within the walls of Reichsburg Castle, a magnificent example of medieval architecture. This itinerary is a treasure trove for history enthusiasts, offering a tangible glimpse into bygone eras at a slightly more budget-friendly price.

Website: https://www.vikingrivercruises.com/cruise-destinations/europe/de stinations/mainz/index.html

The Epicurean Voyage (Estimated Price: $3,000 - $4,000)

For those whose taste buds are their compass, the Rhine River offers a culinary adventure like no other. In Strasbourg, indulge in hearty Alsatian fare and sip Gewürztraminer in a traditional winstub. In Rüdesheim, embark on a decadent chocolate tasting at the Niederberg Monastery, where the secret to heavenly truffles lies hidden. In Miltenberg, learn the art of Franconian baking and sample freshly baked pretzels still warm from the oven. This itinerary is a delectable feast for the senses, perfect for gourmands and wine aficionados seeking a taste of the Rhine's regional specialties, with a price point that falls in the middle.

Website: https://www.vikingrivercruises.com/cruise-destinations/europe/de stinations/strasbourg/index.html

Beyond the Beaten Path (Estimated Price: $2,000 - $3,000)

For those who crave a touch of the unconventional, the Rhine River offers hidden gems waiting to be discovered. In Nijmegen, explore the Netherlands' oldest city, a charming blend of medieval architecture and modern vibrancy. In Worms, delve into the Nibelungen saga, a legendary tale of love, betrayal, and gold, whispered through the ages. In Speyer, marvel at the Romanesque Speyer Cathedral, a UNESCO World Heritage Site and a testament to the region's rich history. This itinerary is for the adventurous spirit, offering a chance to experience the Rhine's lesser-known treasures at a more budget-conscious price.

Website: https://www.vikingrivercruises.com/

Tailoring Your Journey:

Remember, your itinerary is a blank canvas, ready to be painted with your unique desires. Do you crave active adventures? Opt for cycling tours along the riverbank or hikes through the verdant hills. Are you seeking relaxation? Immerse yourself in spa treatments onboard your ship or lose yourself in a good book on a sun-drenched deck. Like the river itself, the options are limitless.

Budgeting and Cost Considerations

Making a budget for your Rhine River vacation requires careful planning. Consider the cost of the cruise, excursions, and onboard charges. Pre-planning and looking for offers and packages will help you maximize your money and ensure a delightful and cost-effective tour along the gorgeous and historic Rhine.

Cruising on a Budget-Friendly Tide:

The cruise itself is your voyage's centerpiece, but its price tag can be daunting. Expect to pay anywhere between €1,200 and €3,500 per person for a standard 7-day cruise during shoulder seasons (spring and fall). Peak season (summer) sees prices climb by 20-30%. To conquer these financial waves, consider:

- **Early booking:** Snag early bird discounts and secure the best cabins before prices rise.
- Shorter cruises: Pack in the highlights on a 3–5-day adventure for a more budget-conscious experience.
- **Interior cabins:** Embrace the coziness (and savings!) of an interior cabin for a significant price drop.
- **Cruise line promotions:** Research deals for seniors, families, and first-time cruisers.

Beyond the Ship: Port of Call Expenses:

While the cruise covers accommodation and most meals, onshore adventures and independent exploration add to the cost. Excursions can range from €40 to €150 per person, depending on the activity. Consider:

- **Independent exploration:** Research your ports and plan adventures using public transportation or walking tours. Many towns offer free historical landmarks and picturesque squares to discover.
- **Sharing excursions:** Team up with fellow travelers to split the cost of larger group tours.
- **Packing picnics:** Enjoy the scenery and save money by packing lunches and snacks for in-between meals.

Dining Delights:

Most cruises include breakfast and dinner, but lunch and specialty dining experiences can add to your tab. Budget around €15-€35 per person for lunch buffets and a la carte options. To avoid exceeding your budget:

- **Limit specialty dinners:** Choose one or two special dining experiences to savor local flavors without breaking the bank.
- **Pack snacks and drinks:** Stock up on essentials like water bottles and snacks to avoid pricey onboard purchases.

Tipping the Scales:

Tipping on Rhine River cruises is customary, though not mandatory. Budget around €5-€8 per person, per day for housekeeping and dining staff. Some cruise lines include gratuities in the fare, so check beforehand.

Hidden Gems of Savings:

Beyond these core expenses, factor in travel insurance, transportation to and from embarkation points, and visa fees (if applicable). To stay afloat financially:

- **Set a daily spending limit:** This helps you track your expenses and avoid overspending.
- **Withdraw cash in advance:** Minimize ATM fees by withdrawing cash before the cruise.
- **Pack travel essentials:** Avoid pricey onboard purchases by packing essentials like sunscreen, water bottles, and comfortable walking shoes.
- **Look for free activities:** Each port offers free attractions like visiting local markets or picnicking along the riverbank.

Charting Your Course:

Remember, your budget is your guide, not a rigid constraint. Prioritize your must-have experiences and adjust accordingly. Seek cheaper alternatives for excursions, utilize public transportation, and savor free attractions. With savvy planning and a touch of flexibility, your Rhine River cruise will be an unforgettable adventure without breaking the bank.

Estimated Prices:

- **Cruise:** €1,200 – €3,500 per person (7-day cruise)
- **Excursions:** €40 – €150 per person
- **Lunch:** €15 – €35 per person
- **Tipping:** €5 – €8 per person, per day
- **Travel Insurance:** Varies depending on coverage
- **Transportation:** Varies depending on location and mode of travel

Remember, these are just estimates, and actual costs may vary depending on your specific choices.

Booking Tips and Deals

Unlock a seamless Rhine River adventure with savvy booking tips and deals. Explore early booking discounts, last-minute offers, and package deals. Leverage loyalty programs and compare prices across various platforms for the best value. Embrace these insights to secure a memorable journey along the historic and scenic Rhine.

Timing is Everything:

- **Early Bird Catches the Deal:** For the best prices and cabin availability, aim to book your Rhine River cruise 6-12 months in advance, especially during peak season (June-August). Shoulder seasons (May, September, and October) offer good deals closer to the departure date.
- **Last-Minute Luck:** If flexibility is your superpower, last-minute deals (2-3 months before departure) can be surprisingly sweet, especially for shorter cruises or sailings outside peak season. Be prepared to be flexible with dates and cabin types.

Deconstructing the Fare:

- **Cabin Categories:** Choose wisely! Inside cabins offer the most budget-friendly option, while riverview and balcony cabins come with a premium price tag. Consider your priorities: is a window essential for soaking in the scenery, or are you content with cozy evenings spent reading in an interior cabin?
- **Cruise Line Choices:** Luxury lines like Emerald Waterways and Scenic cater to discerning palates with all-inclusive packages and plush amenities, while value-oriented lines like Avalon Waterways and Gate 1 Travel offer more affordable options with a focus on exploration.
- **Promotional Prowess:** Keep an eye out for special promotions like "early booking discounts," "two-for-one fares," and onboard credit offers. Cruise lines often advertise these deals on their websites and social media

platforms.

Beyond the Brochure:

- **Consider Group Travel:** Traveling with a group of eight or more can unlock significant discounts on certain cruise lines. Contact cruise lines directly to inquire about group rates.
- **Shore Excursions:** While onboard excursions offer convenience, independent exploration can be budget friendly. Research your ports of call and plan DIY adventures utilizing public transportation, walking tours, or renting bikes.
- **Travel Insurance:** It's always wise to invest in travel insurance for peace of mind. Compare different plans and choose one that covers unexpected cancellations, medical emergencies, and lost luggage

Remember, the Rhine River cruise is more than just a vacation; it's an investment in memories. By using these booking tips and deals, you can craft an unforgettable journey that resonates with both your wanderlust and your wallet.

Chapter 3: Getting Ready for Your Cruise

P repare for an enchanting Rhine River Cruise with essential readiness steps. Pack smartly with key essentials, tick off your pre-cruise checklist for a seamless start, and secure travel insurance while prioritizing health precautions. Ensure a worry-free and delightful journey through the picturesque landscapes along the historic Rhine.

Packing Essentials

Prepare for your Rhine River excursion with these essential packing tips. Ensure you have the correct gear, from weather-resistant apparel to comfortable footwear for expeditions. Don't forget travel basics like adapters and cameras to ensure a flawless and comfortable experience as you tour the scenic delights of the Rhine.

For the Ladies:

Embrace the European flair with versatile pieces that effortlessly transform from daytime explorations to elegant evening soirees. Pack 2-3 comfortable and stylish pairs of walking shoes, ideally one waterproof pair for unpredictable weather. Lightweight jeans, chinos, and flowy skirts provide mix-and-match options, while a dressy pair of pants and a versatile top will elevate your look for formal dinners. Pack layering pieces like lightweight sweaters, cardigans, and scarves to adapt to changing temperatures. A packable rain jacket is your essential shield against sudden showers, while a stylish sun hat protects and adds a touch of Parisian chic. Don't forget a cross-body bag or small backpack for daytime adventures, and a sleek clutch or evening bag for those glamorous galas. Remember, packing cubes are your organizational knights in shining armor!

Essentials Checklist:

- 2-3 pairs comfortable walking shoes (1 waterproof)
- Lightweight jeans, chinos, skirts
- Dressy pants and versatile top
- Lightweight sweaters, cardigans, scarves
- Packable rain jacket
- Stylish sun hat
- Cross-body bag or small backpack
- Sleek clutch or evening bag
- Packing cubes

For the Gentlemen:

Channel your inner European gentleman with a balance of practicality and panache. Pack 2-3 pairs of comfortable walking shoes, including a sturdy pair for potential hikes. Chinos, dark-wash jeans, and light button-down shirts offer versatile daytime attire, while a blazer and dress pants elevate your look for formal evenings. Knit polo shirts and light sweaters add layering options, while a packable rain jacket keeps you dry on unexpected drizzly days. A stylish hat shields you from the sun and adds a touch of continental elegance. Remember, a quality leather belt and a versatile pair of sunglasses complete the sophisticated traveler's ensemble. Don't forget a cross-body bag or backpack for day trips, and a sleek briefcase or dopp kit for more formal settings.

Essentials Checklist:

- 2-3 pairs comfortable walking shoes (1 sturdy)
- Chinos, dark-wash jeans, button-down shirts
- Blazer and dress pants
- Knit polo shirts, light sweaters
- Packable rain jacket
- Stylish hat
- Leather belt, sunglasses
- Cross-body bag or backpack
- Sleek briefcase or dopp kit

For the Kids:

Let their imaginations soar with playful and practical pieces. Pack 2-3 pairs of sturdies, weather-resistant shoes suitable for rambunctious playground adventures and cobblestone explorations. Comfortable play clothes like t-shirts, leggings, and sweatpants will withstand spills and endless games. Don't forget a swimsuit and sun hat for splashing in the Rhine or exploring riverfront towns. Pack lightweight raincoat and warm clothes in case of chilly evenings. To fuel their imaginations, bring along a backpack with coloring books, games, and small toys to keep them entertained onboard and during excursions.

Essentials Checklist:

- 2-3 pairs sturdy, weather-resistant shoes
- Comfortable play clothes (t-shirts, leggings, sweatpants)
- Swimsuit and sun hat
- Lightweight raincoat and warm clothes
- Backpack with coloring books, games, and small toys

Beyond the Basics:

Remember, both ladies and gentlemen should pack comfortable underwear, socks, pajamas, and swimwear. Don't forget essentials like toiletries, sunglasses, sunscreen, a travel adapter, and medications. To remain hydrated and cut down on plastic waste, bring a reusable water bottle with you. For the tech-savvy, a portable charger and headphones are your travel companions. Finally, embrace the unexpected! Throw in a good book, a deck of cards, or a journal to capture the fleeting magic of your Rhine River adventure.

Pro Tips:

· Check dress codes for any formal dinners or special events onboard.
· Pack clothes that can be easily layered for changing weather.
· Roll clothes to save space and prevent wrinkles.
· Leave room in your luggage for souvenirs!

Travel Insurance and Health Precautions

Safeguard your Rhine River adventure with comprehensive travel insurance and health precautions. Ensure coverage for unforeseen events, prioritize health measures, and familiarize yourself with medical facilities along the route. Embrace peace of mind as you cruise, cherishing every moment along the stunning Rhine landscapes.

Securing Your Serenity: Travel Insurance Essentials

Travel insurance becomes your trusted anchor, holding you steady against unforeseen currents like trip cancellations, unexpected medical woes, and lost luggage. Consider these crucial coverage options:

1. **Trip cancellation/interruption:** This shields you financially if unforeseen circumstances, like family emergencies or natural disasters, force you to cancel or prematurely end your trip.
2. **Medical coverage:** Emergency medical expenses abroad can be daunting. Secure adequate coverage for unexpected illnesses or accidents during

your travels.

3. **Evacuation coverage:** Should you require medical evacuation from your cruise ship or port city, this safeguard ensures swift and seamless transportation to a qualified medical facility.

4. **Baggage and personal belongings:** Lost or damaged luggage can cast a shadow over even the sunniest vacation. This coverage provides peace of mind and financial protection for your belongings.

Cost Considerations:

Travel insurance prices vary based on factors like the duration and itinerary of your cruise, your age, and any pre-existing medical conditions. Generally, expect to pay between 5% and 10% of your total trip cost for comprehensive coverage. Consider the peace of mind versus the financial outlay and prioritize robust coverage over cheaper options.

Finding Your Policy Compass:

Don't embark on a quest through a labyrinth of providers. Start by checking with your existing travel insurance provider or homeowner's/renter's insurance policy to see if your trip is already covered. Alternatively, reputable online comparison tools like Squaremouth or InsureMyTrip can help you compare quotes from various insurance companies. Prioritize companies with strong financial ratings and reliable customer service.

Health Precautions: Sailing Towards Well-being:

Beyond safeguarding your finances, prioritize your physical well-being. Here are some crucial health precautions for a healthy Rhine River cruise:

- **Pack essential medications:** Don't rely on finding your specific prescriptions abroad. Pack enough medication for the entire duration of your trip, with a buffer for unexpected delays.

- **Stay up-to-date on vaccinations:** Ensure you're current on all necessary vaccinations, including COVID-19 boosters and any region-specific shots like rabies or tick-borne illness vaccines.
- **Purchase travel health insurance:** Even with domestic health insurance, coverage abroad can be limited. Travel health insurance provides additional peace of mind and ensures access to quality medical care if needed.
- **Pack a travel first-aid kit:** Be prepared for minor ailments with a well-stocked kit containing essentials like pain relievers, bandages, antidiarrheal medication, and antiseptic wipes.
- **Stay informed about health advisories:** Check with your local health department and the Centers for Disease Control and Prevention (CDC) for any travel advisories or specific health concerns in the countries you'll be visiting.

Embrace the Journey with Confidence:

With mindful foresight, adequate travel insurance, and essential health precautions, your Rhine River cruise can be a tapestry woven with carefree laughter, breathtaking landscapes, and memories that shimmer brighter than the river itself. So, bon voyage, fellow traveler! Set sail with your peace of mind in tow, ready to conquer any potential storms and bask in the sun-kissed splendor of your European adventure.

Additional Resources:

- **Centers for Disease Control and Prevention (CDC):** https://wwwnc.cdc.gov/travel
- **World Health Organization (WHO):** https://www.who.int/travel-advice
- **Travel Insurance Association of America (TIAA):** https://www.tiaa.org/public/invest/services/wealth-management/travelinsurance

Remember, these are just general recommendations. Always consult with your doctor and research insurance options based on your specific needs and itinerary.

Local Transportation Options

Trains: Your Iron Steed Through Time:

Imagine hurtling past vineyards in Germany, castles in Switzerland, and windmills in the Netherlands – all from the comfort of a modern train. Trains are the backbone of European travel, offering efficient connections between major towns like Cologne (Köln Hauptbahnhof, Trankgasse 1, 50667 Köln, Germany), Strasbourg (Gare Centrale de Strasbourg, Place de l'Étoile, 67000 Strasbourg, France), and Basel (Bahnhof Basel SBB, Centralbahnstrasse 21, 4005 Basel, Switzerland).

- **Booking:** Plan your journey and book tickets online on national railway websites like https://int.bahn.de/en: https://int.bahn.de/en (Germany), https://www.sbb.ch/en: https://www.sbb.ch/en (Switzerland), and https://www.nsinternational.com/en: https://www.nsinternational.com/en (Netherlands).
- **Payment:** Purchase tickets with credit cards or cash at ticket machines or counters.
- **Cost:** Prices vary depending on distance and class, but expect to pay around €15-€30 for short journeys.
- **Conditions:** Modern, comfortable, and punctual, European trains are a joy to ride.
- **Challenges:** Timetables may change seasonally, so check schedules beforehand. Large luggage can be cumbersome on crowded trains.

Buses: Venturing Off the Beaten Track:

While not as extensive as trains, buses connect smaller towns and villages, offering access to hidden treasures like Rüdesheim's charming Drosselgasse (Drosselgasse 10, 65375 Rüdesheim am Rhein, Germany) or the quaint wine village of Cochem (Marktplatz 1, 56812 Cochem, Germany). Imagine discovering a medieval gem nestled amidst rolling hills, accessible only by a local bus.

- **Booking:** Tickets are usually purchased on board or at bus stops.
- **Payment:** Cash is the preferred method, although some buses accept cards.
- **Cost:** Prices are generally affordable, often just a few euros per journey.
- **Conditions:** Buses may be less frequent than trains and can be crowded during peak season.
- **Challenges:** Limited English signage and announcements may be encountered. Consider downloading translation apps like Google Translate for assistance.

Taxis: Door-to-Door Convenience:

For a touch of luxury and convenience, grab a taxi to explore vibrant cities like Cologne's bustling Altstadt (Old Town) (Heumarkt 32, 50667 Köln, Germany) or Amsterdam's picturesque canals. Imagine whisking through charming lanes, arriving at your destination refreshed and ready to explore.

- **Booking:** Hail taxis on the street, call a taxi company, or use ride-hailing apps like Uber.
- **Payment:** Cash is the most common method, but some accept credit cards.
- **Cost:** Expect to pay around €10-€20 for short journeys, depending on distance and time of day.
- **Conditions:** Taxis are generally reliable and comfortable.
- **Challenges:** Language barriers may be encountered, so having basic phrases in the local language handy is helpful.

Bicycles: Two Wheels, Endless Freedom:

For the adventurous souls, renting a bike offers an exhilarating way to explore the Rhine Valley. Imagine pedaling along scenic paths like the Rhine Cycle Route (Rheinradweg), stopping to admire vineyards and charming villages at your own pace. Cycle past the majestic Lorelei rock (Loreleyfelsen, 56346 St. Goarshausen, Germany) or explore the enchanting Black Forest region (Freudenstadt Marktplatz, Marktplatz 2, 72270 Freudenstadt, Germany) on two wheels.

- **Booking:** Rent bikes from local shops or online platforms like https://www.bajabikes.eu/ or https://www.getyourguide.com/, which offer rental locations across major cities along the Rhine.
- **Payment:** Pay with credit cards or cash at the rental shop.
- **Cost:** Prices vary depending on bike type and rental duration, typically €10-€20 per day.
- **Conditions:** The Rhine Valley boasts extensive cycling paths, offering safe and scenic routes. Some sections might involve hilly terrain, so prepare accordingly.
- **Challenges:** Be aware of traffic regulations and ensure you have proper safety equipment like helmets and reflective clothing. Consider purchasing a bike map or downloading route-planning apps like Komoot or Strava.

Navigating the System:

- **Plan ahead:** Research local transportation options and schedules before your cruise, especially if venturing beyond major towns.
- **Download maps and apps:** Google Maps and local public transport apps can be your lifesavers. Many cities offer dedicated apps for their transport networks.
- **Learn basic phrases:** Knowing a few words in German, French, or Dutch will go a long way.
- **Validate your tickets:** Be sure to validate tickets on buses and trams before boarding.
- **Carry cash:** Some local buses and shops may not accept cards.
- **Ask for help:** Don't hesitate to ask locals or tourist information centers

for assistance. Most people are happy to help, especially if you try a few words in their language.

Chapter 4: Rhine River Highlights

E xplore the Rhine River's captivating features on a Rhine River adventure. Admire the gorgeous landscapes and historic landmarks that dot the riverbanks. Immerse yourself in cultural and historical treasures, uncovering stories of ancient legends and modern-day delights along this scenic canal, ensuring an interesting and memorable cruise experience.

Scenic Views and Landmarks

Prepare to be wowed by the Rhine River's stunning beautiful panoramas and historic landmarks. From the magnificent Lorelei Rock to the lovely Rhine Gorge, be enchanted by attractive towns, luscious vineyards, and historic castles, all of which promise an awe-inspiring ride down this picturesque waterway.

1. Cologne Cathedral (Kölner Dom): This colossal Gothic masterpiece dominates Cologne's skyline and is a UNESCO World Heritage Site. Soaring spires pierce the sky, and intricate stained-glass windows bathe the interior in a kaleidoscope of colors.

Location: Domkloster 4, 50677 Köln, Germany

Website: https://www.koelner-dom.de/en

- **Historical background:** Construction began in 1248 and spanned over 600 years, making it a testament to human ambition and faith.
- **Curiosity:** The cathedral houses the Shrine of the Three Kings, believed to hold the remains of the Magi.
- **Practical information:** Open daily, with free admission to the nave. Guided tours and tickets to climb the towers are available.
- **What to do and see:** Explore the intricate carvings, marvel at the stained-glass windows, and climb the towers for panoramic views of Cologne.
- **Outdoor advice:** Wear comfortable shoes for exploring the cathedral and surrounding area.
- **Entrance fee:** Free (nave), €12 (towers), €6 (guided tour)
- **Helpful tip:** Avoid visiting during peak tourist season (July–August) to skip long queues.
- **How to get there:** Cologne is easily accessible by train, plane, or car. The cathedral is a short walk from the main train station.

2. Rhine Gorge: This UNESCO World Heritage Site is a dramatic stretch of the river, where steep cliffs cloaked in lush forests rise dramatically from the water. Dotted with charming villages, ancient castles, and vineyards, the Rhine Gorge is a landscape painter's dream.

Location: Between Wiesbaden and Bonn, Germany

Website: https://whc.unesco.org/en/list/1066/

- **Historical background:** Formed by millions of years of erosion, the gorge was a vital trade route for centuries.
- **Curiosity:** The Lorelei, a mythical siren said to lure sailors to their doom, is associated with a particularly treacherous stretch of the gorge.
- **Practical information:** Best explored by boat, train, or car. Numerous hiking trails offer stunning viewpoints.
- **What to do and see:** Take a boat cruise, hike the Rheinsteig trail, visit charming towns like Rüdesheim and Oberwesel, or explore the ruins of

medieval castles like Rheinfels and Marksburg.
- **Outdoor advice:** Wear sturdy shoes for hiking, pack sunscreen and water, and be mindful of potential landslides, especially after heavy rain.
- **Entrance fee:** Free (hiking trails), varies for boat cruises and castles
- Helpful tip: Purchase a Rhine Pass for discounted travel on trains and boats throughout the gorge.
- **How to get there:** Train stations and boat piers are located in towns along the gorge.

3. Heidelberg Castle: This imposing red sandstone castle perched atop a hill overlooks the picturesque city of Heidelberg. A symbol of German Romanticism, the castle boasts stunning architecture, beautiful gardens, and a fascinating history.

Location: Schloss Heidelberg, 69115 Heidelberg, Germany

Website: https://www.schloss-heidelberg.de/en/

- **Historical background:** The castle dates back to the 13th century and has served as a residence for Electors Palatine, a university, and a military base.
- **Curiosity:** The Heidelberg Tun, a giant wooden barrel once used to store wine, is now a popular tourist attraction.
- **Practical information:** Open daily, with guided tours and self-guided exploration options available.
- **What to do and see:** Explore the castle halls and courtyards, admire the panoramic views from the terrace, stroll through the gardens, and visit the Heidelberg Tun.
- **Outdoor advice:** Wear comfortable shoes for walking uphill and be prepared for crowds during peak season.
- **Entrance fee:** €12 (adults), €6 (children)
- **Helpful tip:** Arrive early to avoid long lines, especially for guided tours.
- **How to get there:** Heidelberg is easily accessible by train or car. The city

center is a short stroll from the castle.

4. Rüdesheim am Rhein: This charming town on the east bank of the Rhine is a delightful mix of medieval architecture, quaint streets, and vineyards. The Drosselgasse, a narrow alley lined with half-timbered houses, is a must-see, while the Niederwald Monument offers stunning views of the surrounding valley.

Website: https://www.ruedesheim.de/

- **Curiosity:** Rüdesheim is known for its production of Riesling wine, and visitors can enjoy tastings at local wineries.
- **Practical information:** Easily accessible by train, boat, or car. Explore the town on foot, take a boat cruise, or hop on the Niederwaldbahn, a funicular railway to the monument.
- **What to do and see:** Stroll through the Drosselgasse, visit the Siegfried Mechanical Music Museum, admire the Niederwald Monument, and enjoy wine tastings in local cellars.
- **Outdoor advice:** Wear comfortable shoes for walking, and pack sunscreen and a hat during summer.
- **Entrance fee:** Free (town, Drosselgasse), €5 (Niederwald Monument), varies for museums and wineries
- **Helpful tip:** Visit during the Rüdesheimer Weinfest (September) for a lively celebration of wine and local culture.
- **How to get there:** Train stations and boat piers are located in Rüdesheim.

5. Marksburg Castle: This imposing hilltop fortress, perched high above the Rhine near Braubach, is the only medieval castle in the Rhine Gorge that has never been destroyed. Its well-preserved towers, ramparts, and courtyards offer a glimpse into medieval life.

Location: Marksburg 1, 56322 Braubach, Germany

Website: https://www.marksburg.de/

- **Historical background:** Constructed in the 13th century, Marksburg served as a refuge for royalty and a military stronghold for centuries.
- **Curiosity:** The castle's thick walls and ingenious defense mechanisms ensured its survival through numerous wars and sieges.
- **Practical information:** Open daily, with guided tours and self-guided exploration options available.
- **What to do and see:** Explore the castle's interior, learn about its history on a guided tour, walk the ramparts for stunning views, and visit the castle museum.
- **Outdoor advice:** Wear comfortable shoes for climbing uphill, and be prepared for crowds during peak season.
- **Entrance fee:** €12 (adults), €6 (children)
- **Helpful tip:** Combine your visit to Marksburg with a boat cruise on the Rhine for a full experience of the gorge's beauty.
- **How to get there:** Marksburg is accessible by car or bus from Braubach. A short hike from the village leads to the castle.
- By exploring these five scenic views and landmarks, you'll experience the magic of the Rhine River. From breathtaking landscapes to charming towns and historical treasures, the Rhine offers a journey through time and beauty.

Additional tips for your Rhine River journey:

- **Consider a Rhine River cruise:** This offers a comfortable and scenic way to experience the river and its landmarks.
- **Learn some basic German phrases:** This will help you connect with locals and enhance your experience.
- **Respect the environment:** Leave no trace and be mindful of local customs and traditions.
- **Pack for all weather conditions:** The Rhine region can experience rain and sunshine, so be prepared for both.

- **Embrace the slow pace:** Relax, savor the scenery, and enjoy the unique charm of the Rhine River.

Cultural and Historical Insights

Explore the Rhine River's unique tapestry of cultural and historical wonders. Discover medieval castles, Gothic cathedrals, and quaint communities steeped in history. Discover the legacies of several civilizations, from Roman remnants to romantic stories, on an interactive trip through centuries of fascinating heritage.

1. Cologne Chocolate Museum (Schokoladenmuseum): This Willy Wonka-esque haven in Cologne isn't just for sweet tooths. It's a time capsule of chocolate's fascinating journey, from Mayan origins to modern-day indulgence.

Location: Schokoladenmuseum, Im Schokoladenmuseum 1-2, 50678 Köln, Germany

Website: https://www.schokoladenmuseum.de/?lang=en

- **Historical background:** Tracing chocolate's evolution from a sacred beverage to a global phenomenon, the museum showcases historical artifacts, interactive exhibits, and live chocolate-making demonstrations.
- **Curiosity:** The museum houses the world's largest chocolate fountain, cascading 15 meters of pure cocoa bliss.
- **Practical information:** Open daily, with guided tours and self-guided exploration options available.
- **What to do and see:** Learn about the history and production of chocolate, witness live chocolate-making demonstrations, indulge in tastings, and create your own personalized chocolate bar.
- **Outdoor advice:** Wear comfortable shoes for exploring the museum and surrounding area.

- **Entrance fee:** €12 (adults), €6 (children)
- **Helpful tip:** Combine your visit with a stroll through Cologne's Old Town and a stop at the iconic Kölner Dom cathedral.
- **How to get there:** Easily accessible by train, plane, or car. The museum is a short walk from the main train station.

2. Gutenberg Museum (Gutenberg-Museum): In Mainz, step back to the dawn of the printing revolution at the Gutenberg Museum. Immerse yourself in the world of Johannes Gutenberg, the inventor of the movable type printing press, and witness the transformative power of the written word.

Location: Gutenberg-Museum, Liebfrauenplatz 5, 55116 Mainz, Germany

Website: https://www.mainz.de/microsite/gutenberg-museum-en/index.php

- **Historical background:** The museum houses the Gutenberg Bible, one of the first printed books ever made, and showcases printing presses, typefaces, and other historical artifacts.
- **Curiosity:** Gutenberg's revolutionary invention democratized knowledge and laid the foundation for modern mass communication.
- **Practical information:** Open daily, with guided tours and self-guided exploration options available.
- **What to do and see:** Explore the history of printing, witness demonstrations of printing with a Gutenberg press, admire the Gutenberg Bible, and discover the impact of printing on society.
- **Outdoor advice:** Wear comfortable shoes for exploring the museum and charming Mainz Old Town.
- **Entrance fee:** €8 (adults), €4 (children)
- **Helpful tip:** Time your visit to coincide with the Gutenberg Festival in July for a vibrant celebration of printing and its legacy.
- **How to get there:** Easily accessible by train or car. The museum is located in the heart of Mainz Old Town.

3. Eltz Castle (Burg Eltz): Perched on a rocky crag amidst lush greenery, Eltz Castle is a fairytale come to life. This 12th-century marvel, untouched by wars, offers a glimpse into medieval life and architecture.

Location: Burg Eltz 67, 56281 Wierschem, Germany

Website: https://burg-eltz.de/en/homepage

- **Historical background:** Built by the Eltz family, the castle passed down through generations and remains privately owned to this day.
- **Curiosity:** The castle's secluded location and intricate architecture, with its gabled towers and colorful facades, have inspired countless artists and writers.
- **Practical information:** Accessible by shuttle bus from the village of Wierschem or by a scenic hike through the forest. Guided tours are available.
- **What to do and see:** Explore the castle's interior, admire the grand halls, knights' chambers, and armory, and soak in the breathtaking views of the surrounding valley.
- **Outdoor advice:** Wear sturdy shoes for the hike or shuttle bus ride and be prepared for crowds during peak season.
- **Entrance fee:** €12.50 (adults), €8 (children)
- **Helpful tip:** Combine your visit to Eltz Castle with a hike in the surrounding hills for an immersive experience of the Mosel Valley's natural beauty.
- **How to get there:** Train to Cochem or Bullay, followed by a bus or taxi to Wierschem.

4. Rüdesheim am Rhein: This charming town on the east bank of the Rhine isn't just about picturesque half-timbered houses and delicious Riesling wine. It's also a treasure trove of cultural heritage, evident in the Drosselgasse, a narrow alley lined with historical buildings, and the Siegfried Mechanical Music Museum.

Location: Rüdesheim am Rhein, Germany

Website: https://www.ruedesheim.de/: https://www.ruedesheim.de/

- **Historical background:** Rüdesheim's strategic location on the Rhine made it a vital trading center for centuries, attracting merchants, artists, and musicians.
- **Curiosity:** The Drosselgasse, once a bustling market street, is now lined with shops and restaurants, offering a glimpse into traditional German life.
- **Practical information:** Easily accessible by train, boat, or car. Explore the town on foot, take a boat cruise, or hop on the Niederwaldbahn, a funicular railway to the Niederwald Monument.
- **What to do and see:** Stroll through the Drosselgasse, visit the Siegfried Mechanical Music Museum with its collection of self-playing instruments, and enjoy wine tastings in local cellars.
- **Outdoor advice:** Wear comfortable shoes for walking and pack sunscreen and a hat during summer.
- **Entrance fee:** Free (Drosselgasse, town), €5 (Niederwald Monument), varies for museums and wineries
- **Helpful tip:** Visit during the Rüdesheimer Weinfest (September) for a lively celebration of wine and local culture.
- **How to get there:** Train stations and boat piers are located in Rüdesheim.

5. **Cochem:** Nestled in a bend of the Mosel River, Cochem is a charming town with a rich history. Explore the impressive Reichsburg, a hilltop castle overlooking the town, and wander through the quaint streets lined with half-timbered houses.

Location: Cochem, Germany

Website: https://www.cochem.de/: https://www.cochem.de/

- **Historical background:** Cochem was once ruled by French and German nobility, leaving behind a legacy of architectural styles and cultural influences.
- **Curiosity:** The Reichsburg, destroyed and rebuilt several times throughout history, offers stunning views of the Mosel Valley and a glimpse into medieval life.
- **Practical information:** Easily accessible by train or car. Explore the town on foot, take a boat cruise on the Mosel, or visit the Reichsburg.
- **What to do and see:** Explore the Reichsburg, wander through the charming Old Town, visit the Cochem Castle wine cellar, and take a boat cruise on the Mosel River.
- **Outdoor advice:** Wear comfortable shoes for walking and climbing the hill to the Reichsburg.
- **Entrance fee:** €7 (Reichsburg), varies for boat cruises and wineries
- **Helpful tip:** Combine your visit to Cochem with a hike in the surrounding hills for breathtaking views of the Mosel Valley.
- **How to get there:** Train to Cochem or Bullay, followed by a bus or taxi to the town center.

Remember:

- Respect local customs and traditions.
- Support local businesses by shopping and eating at independently owned establishments.
- Be mindful of your environmental impact and leave no trace.
- Pack for all weather conditions, as the Rhine region can experience a variety of climates.
- Most importantly, relax, savor the moment, and create lasting memories of your unforgettable Rhine River adventure.

Chapter 5: Life Onboard

E levate your Rhine River cruise experience with insights into onboard life. Discover diverse river cruise ships, luxurious cabins, and enticing amenities. Delight in local cuisine and special dining events. Indulge in onboard entertainment, spa facilities, and activities. Maximize your cruise journey with tips ensuring a seamless and enriching exploration along the scenic Rhine.

Types of River Cruise Ships

Begin your Rhine River experience by learning about the various cruise ships available. Explore a variety of alternatives, from tiny riverboats that inspire camaraderie to grandiose vessels with rich facilities. Discover the ideal balance of comfort and style for a personalized and pleasurable trip along the scenic Rhine.

The Boutique Charm:

For those seeking intimacy and personalized service, smaller ships (carrying around 120 - 160 passengers) are your haven. Imagine cozy onboard atmospheres, spacious sun decks, and a chance to get acquainted with fellow cruisers and crew. Companies like:

- **Emerald Cruises:** https://www.emeraldcruises.com/river-cruises
- **Uniworld Boutique River Cruises:** https://www.uniworld.com/

- **Scenic Luxury Cruises & Tours:** https://www.scenic.com.au/

offer exquisite service, gourmet dining in intimate settings, and thoughtfully curated shore excursions. Expect cabin fees to range from €4,000 - €7,000 per person, depending on cabin category and itinerary.

The Classic Comfort:

For those who value spaciousness and a lively onboard atmosphere, mid-sized ships (carrying around 160 - 250 passengers) are the perfect blend. Think panoramic lounges, expansive sun decks, swimming pools, and varied entertainment options. Companies like:

- **Viking River Cruises:** https://www.vikingcruises.com/oceans
- **AmaWaterways:** https://www.amawaterways.com/
- **Avalon Waterways:** https://www.avalonwaterways.com/

offer a balance of onboard activities and shore excursions, catering to a broader range of preferences. Cabin fees can range from €3,000 - €6,000 per person, depending on cabin category and itinerary.

The Grand Adventure:

For those who crave a bustling hub of activity and endless entertainment, larger ships (carrying around 250 - 350 passengers) are your playground. Imagine cascading decks, multiple dining venues, Broadway-style shows, and even casinos. Companies like:

- **A-ROSA River Cruises:** https://www.a-rosa.de/flusskreuzfahrten.html (German address only: A-ROSA Flusskreuzfahrten GmbH, Brüningstraße 15, 28195 Bremen, Germany)
- **Crystal River Cruises:** https://www.crystalcruises.com/
- **River Line:** https://www.rivercruise-line.eu/

offer the ultimate in onboard amenities and cater to those seeking a social and festive atmosphere. Cabin fees can range from €2,500 - €5,000 per person, depending on cabin category and itinerary.

Beyond the Numbers:

Remember, size is just one factor. Consider amenities like spa facilities, fitness centers, and onboard entertainment that resonate with your interests. Research the dining options and shore excursions offered by each company to ensure they align with your preferences. Finally, consider your budget and choose a ship within your comfort zone.

Additional Tips:

· Consider booking early, especially for smaller ships and peak season, to secure desired cabins and cabins.
· Check for promotional offers and discounts, especially for first-time cruisers or longer itineraries.
· Read online reviews from previous passengers to get a firsthand feel for the atmosphere and experience on different ships.

Cabin Options and Amenities

Enhance your Rhine River cruise by choosing the perfect cabin. From cozy staterooms to luxurious suites, explore diverse options catering to comfort and style. Dive into onboard amenities, ensuring a delightful stay with personalized services, scenic views, and a relaxing retreat after exploring the enchanting Rhine landscapes.

1. Standard Riverview Cabin: Your cozy haven, nestled amidst the heart of the ship. These cabins offer comfortable twin beds (convertible to a king), ample storage space, and a picture window framing the ever-changing Rhine panorama. Ideal for budget-conscious explorers who prioritize restful sleep and convenient access to onboard amenities.

- **Size:** 150 - 180 sq. ft.
- **Amenities:** Private bathroom with shower, TV, mini-fridge, complimentary toiletries.
- **Price Range:** €2,000 - €3,000 per person (7-day cruise)
- **Examples:** Viking River Cruises (https://www.vikingcruises.com/), AmaWaterways (https://www.amawaterways.com/), Avalon Waterways (https://www.avalonwaterways.com/)

2. Deluxe Riverview Cabin: Step into a haven of spacious comfort. These cabins offer generous square footage, plush bedding, and a larger picture window, immersing you in the Rhine's breathtaking beauty. Perfect for couples seeking a touch of luxury and ample space to unwind after exploring charming towns.

- **Size:** 180 - 220 sq. ft.
- **Amenities:** King-sized bed or two twin beds, private bathroom with shower and bathtub, TV, mini-fridge, larger window, upgraded toiletries.
- **Price Range:** €3,000 - €4,000 per person (7-day cruise)
- **Examples:** Emerald Cruises (https://www.emeraldcruises.com/river-cruises), Uniworld Boutique River Cruises (https://www.uniworld.com/), Scenic Luxury Cruises & Tours (https://www.scenic.com.au/)

3. Balcony Cabin: Embrace the ultimate indulgence. These cabins boast a private balcony, your own open-air stage to savor the Rhine's magic. Sip your morning coffee while watching sunlight dance on ancient castles, or enjoy a glass of wine under a starlit sky. Ideal for romantics and nature lovers seeking an immersive experience.

- **Size:** 180 - 250 sq. ft. (including balcony)
- **Amenities:** King-sized bed or two twin beds, private bathroom with shower and bathtub, TV, mini-fridge, balcony with chairs and table,

upgraded toiletries.
- **Price Range:** €4,000 - €5,000 per person (7-day cruise)
- **Examples:** A-ROSA River Cruises (https://www.arosa-cruises.com/river-cruises.html), Crystal River Cruises (https://www.crystalcruises.com/), River Line (https://www.rivercruise-line.eu/)

4. Suite: Unleash your inner royalty. Suites offer the pinnacle of river cruise accommodation. Spacious living areas, luxurious bathrooms with whirlpool tubs, and some even boast private terraces. Ideal for discerning travelers seeking unparalleled comfort, privacy, and exclusive amenities like in-suite dining and priority embarkation.

- **Size:** 300 - 500 sq. ft.
- **Amenities:** King-sized bed, separate living room, private bathroom with whirlpool tub, TV, mini-bar, balcony or private terrace with furniture, upgraded toiletries, priority boarding, in-suite dining options (on some ships).
- **Price Range:** €6,000 - €10,000 per person (7-day cruise)
- **Examples:** Crystal River Cruises, Scenic Luxury Cruises & Tours, Emerald Cruise

5. Single Cabin: Solo travelers, rejoice! No need to compromise comfort or miss out on the Rhine River magic. Many cruise lines offer dedicated single cabins, designed for comfort and convenience. Enjoy your own cozy haven without a single supplement.

- **Size:** 120 - 150 sq. ft.
- **Amenities:** Twin bed or queen-sized bed, private bathroom with shower, TV, mini-fridge, ample storage space, sometimes with a window (availability varies by ship).
- **Price Range:** €2,500 - €3,500 per person (7-day cruise)
- **Examples:** Viking River Cruises, AmaWaterways, Avalon Waterways

Remember, size is just one factor. Consider your budget, desired level of privacy, and preferred amenities. Do you crave a balcony for fresh air and breathtaking views? Do you prioritize a spacious living area for relaxation? Tailor your choice to your unique travel style and preferences.

Dining Options

Savor the essence of the Rhine River through its delectable dining offerings onboard. Immerse yourself in local cuisine, a culinary journey reflecting the region's flavors. Experience special dining events that elevate your gastronomic adventure, ensuring a delightful fusion of culture and exquisite tastes throughout your cruise along this historic waterway.

1. The Grand Opera: The Main Dining Room:

This elegant space sets the stage for your culinary journey. Breakfast buffets brimming with fresh pastries, local cheeses, and smoked salmon awaken your senses. Lunchtime unfolds a rotating menu of regional specialties, from hearty German sausages to creamy French quiches. Dinner becomes a grand affair, with multi-course creations showcasing the finest seasonal ingredients and the chef's artistry.

- **Location:** Main deck, readily accessible from most cabins.
- **Atmosphere:** Elegant, sophisticated, with attentive service.
- **Typical Menu:** Regional specialties, international classics, vegetarian options, à la carte choices available.
- **Included in Fare:** Yes, all meals in the main dining room are included in most cruise packages.

Examples: Viking River Cruises (https://www.vikingcruises.com/), AmaWaterways (https://www.amawaterways.com/), Avalon Waterways (https://www.avalonwaterways.com/)

2. The Intimate Interlude: The Specialty Restaurant:

Crave exclusivity? Many cruise lines offer specialty restaurants. Savor a gourmet French tasting menu paired with perfectly chosen wines at Crystal River Cruises (https://www.crystalcruises.com/), or indulge in a succulent Italian feast with fresh pasta and melt-in-your-mouth tiramisu at Scenic Luxury Cruises & Tours (https://www.scenic.com.au/). Reservations are essential, as these intimate settings fill up quickly.

- **Location:** Varies by ship, often on a higher deck with panoramic views.
- **Atmosphere:** Romantic, intimate, with personalized service.
- **Typical Menu:** Regional specialties, gourmet dishes, fixed-price menus, à la carte options.
- **Included in Fare:** Varies by cruise line, some offer specialty dining as an optional extra, while others include one or two nights in the specialty restaurant.

3. The Casual Encore: The Café or Grill:

Sometimes, a casual bite and refreshing beverage hit the spot. The onboard café or grill offers a relaxed atmosphere with lighter fare like sandwiches, salads, pizzas, and grilled specialties. Perfect for a quick lunch between shore excursions or a late-night snack under the stars at A-ROSA River Cruises (https://www.a-rosa.de/flusskreuzfahrten.html) or River Line (https://www.rivercruise-line.eu/).

- **Location:** Often on a lower deck with easy access to the sun deck.
- **Atmosphere:** Casual, relaxed, with self-service options.
- **Typical Menu:** Sandwiches, salads, pizzas, grilled dishes, coffee, tea, snacks.
- **Included in Fare:** Varies by cruise line, some items may be included, while others may have additional charges.

4. The Sweet Harmony: Room Service:

For a truly private dining experience, savor the comfort of your cabin. Most cruise lines offer room service, allowing you to indulge in breakfast in bed, a romantic candlelit dinner at AmaWaterways or a late-night snack without leaving your sanctuary at Viking River Cruises or Avalon Waterways.

- **Location:** Delivered directly to your cabin.
- **Atmosphere:** Private, intimate, with personalized service.
- **Typical Menu:** Limited menu of sandwiches, salads, soups, desserts, and beverages.
- **Included in Fare:** Varies by cruise line, some may offer limited room service options for free, while others may have additional charges.

5. The Pop-Up Palate: Themed Events and Tastings:

Many cruise lines elevate your dining experience with special events and tastings. Enjoy a cheese and wine pairing on the sun deck while watching the sunset paint the Rhine, participate in a cooking demonstration showcasing regional specialties, or attend a beer tasting aboard a docked barge at A-ROSA River Cruises or River Line. These pop-up events offer a delightful and interactive way to delve deeper into European flavors.

- **Location:** Varies by event, could be the sun deck, lounge, or even a docked barge.
- **Atmosphere:** Fun, interactive, with opportunities to learn and socialize.
- **Typical Offerings:** Cheese and wine tastings, cooking demonstrations, beer tastings, regional specialty tastings.
- **Included in Fare:** Some events may be included, while others may have additional charges.

6. The Sweet Finale: Afternoon Tea:

Embrace a touch of British elegance with afternoon tea. Indulge in delicate finger sandwiches, fluffy scones with clotted cream and jam, and an array of delectable pastries. Often paired with live music or stunning river views, this delightful ritual is the perfect way to unwind after a day of exploring charming towns and medieval castles.

- **Location:** Lounge or designated area on the ship.
- **Atmosphere:** Refined, relaxed, with a touch of formality.
- **Typical Offerings:** Finger sandwiches, scones with clotted cream and jam, pastries, tea, coffee, sometimes champagne.
- **Included in Fare:** Sometimes included, sometimes available for an additional fee.

Onboard Entertainment and Activities

Enrich your Rhine River cruise with a plethora of onboard entertainment and activities. From cultural performances to engaging lectures, immerse yourself in the charm of the region. Whether unwinding with spa treatments or participating in exciting events, every moment onboard promises to enhance your cruise experience along the picturesque Rhine.

1. The Stage Unfolds: Live Performances and Entertainment

Embrace the magic of live entertainment. Settle into the elegant theater and be captivated by Broadway-style shows, classical music concerts, or local folk ensembles at Crystal River Cruises https://www.crystalcruises.com/ or Scenic Luxury Cruises & Tours https://www.scenic.com.au/. Smaller ships may offer intimate jazz evenings or lively singalongs in the lounge. No need to book tickets, let the music wash over you and discover hidden talents among your fellow passengers.

- **Location:** Theater, lounge, or outdoor deck (weather permitting).
- **Atmosphere:** Varies from elegant and formal to casual and interactive.

- **Typical Performances:** Broadway-style shows, classical music concerts, folk or regional music ensembles, guest speakers, movie nights.
- **Included in Fare:** Yes, all main onboard entertainment is included in most cruise packages.

2. The Game's Afoot: Active Pursuits and Fitness

Stay agile and invigorated. Take a dip in the refreshing pool on a sunny afternoon, challenge yourself with onboard fitness classes at Viking River Cruises https://www.vikingcruises.com/ or AmaWaterways https://www.ama waterways.com/ ranging from Pilates to Zumba, or join a walking group along the picturesque riverbank. Some ships even offer onboard mini-golf courses or shuffleboard courts at A-ROSA River Cruises https://www.a-rosa.de/flussk reuzfahrten.html or River Line https://www.rivercruise-line.eu/.

- **Location:** Pool deck, fitness center, outdoor walking path (sometimes), dedicated game areas.
- **Atmosphere:** Energetic, fun, and social.
- **Typical Activities:** Swimming, fitness classes, hiking, biking excursions, walking groups, onboard games, mini-golf, shuffleboard.
- **Included in Fare:** Pool access and basic fitness classes are usually included; some specialized classes or excursions may have additional fees.

3. The Mind Awakens: Cultural Enrichment and Lectures

Delve deeper into the history and culture of the regions you're exploring. Attend informative lectures by guest speakers, ranging from local historians to art experts, at Emerald Cruises https://www.emeraldcruises.com/river -cruises or Uniworld Boutique River Cruises https://www.uniworld.com/. Participate in wine tastings showcasing regional vintages, learn traditional German dances, or take a language class, opportunities abound to expand your knowledge and understanding of the places you visit.

- **Location:** Library, lounge, or designated lecture room.
- **Atmosphere:** Engaging, educational, and interactive.
- **Typical Activities:** Guest lectures, wine tastings, cooking demonstrations, language classes, cultural workshops, local music lessons.
- **Included in Fare:** Many lectures and basic cultural activities are included; some specialized workshops or tastings may have additional fees.

4. The Social Butterfly Emerges: Mingling and Making Memories

Cruise life thrives on connections. Mingle with fellow travelers over cocktails in the bar, participate in themed onboard parties, or join trivia nights and game shows. Some ships even host onboard talent shows or offer formal galas at Avalon Waterways https://www.avalonwaterways.com/ – perfect opportunities to break the ice and create lasting friendships.

- **Location:** Bar, lounge, open decks, designated event spaces.
- **Atmosphere:** Fun, social, and interactive.
- **Typical Activities:** Cocktail parties, themed evenings, trivia nights, game shows, talent shows, formal galas.
- **Included in Fare:** Most social events are included; some specialty cocktails or private parties may have additional fees.

5. The Sanctuary Beckons: Quiet Contemplation and Relaxation

Embrace moments of serenity amidst the vibrant activity. Curl up with a good book in the sun-drenched library, find your zen in a dedicated meditation space at A-ROSA River Cruises or River Line, or unwind with a rejuvenating spa treatment at Scenic Luxury Cruises & Tours or Crystal River Cruises. Some ships even offer open-air sundecks equipped with loungers and blankets, perfect for stargazing on clear nights.

- **Location:** Library, meditation space, spa, sun deck.
- **Atmosphere:** Peaceful, tranquil, and restorative.

- **Typical Activities:** Reading, meditation, yoga, spa treatments, sun-bathing, stargazing.
- **Included in Fare:** Access to the library and sundeck is usually included, spa treatments and some yoga classes may have additional fees.

Remember, onboard life extends beyond organized activities. Strike up conversations with the crew, delve into historical books in the library, or simply sit on the deck and watch the world glide by. Your Rhine River cruise is an invitation to personalize your experience, to find your own rhythm of relaxation and discovery.

Spa and Wellness Facilities

Enjoy onboard rejuvenation with luxury spa and wellness facilities while cruising along the Rhine. Pamper yourself with luxurious treatments, unwind with tranquil vistas, and revel in the ultimate in relaxation. Enhance your sailing experience by relaxing your mind and body in the quiet flow of the river.

1. Indulge in Tranquility: The Spa Sanctuary

Immerse yourself in a soothing haven dedicated to pampering. Most ships boast spacious spa areas equipped with saunas, steam rooms, and whirlpool baths. Some, like those on Viking River Cruises https://www.vikingcruises.com/ and AmaWaterways https://www.amawaterways.com/, even offer salt therapy rooms to promote deeper relaxation and respiratory benefits. Unwind after a day of exploring charming towns, let the gentle heat soothe your muscles, and emerge feeling invigorated and ready for your next adventure.

- **Location:** Dedicated spa area, often on a higher deck with scenic views.
- **Atmosphere:** Tranquil, luxurious, and restorative.
- **Typical Facilities:** Saunas, steam rooms, whirlpool baths, salt therapy rooms (on some ships), relaxation lounges.

- **Included in Fare**: Access to the spa facilities is usually included in most cruise packages.
- **Examples:** Viking River Cruises, AmaWaterways, Avalon Waterways https://www.avalonwaterways.com/

2. Embrace Pampering: Treatments for Every Need

Indulge in a menu of therapeutic delights designed to rejuvenate both body and spirit. Skilled therapists offer a range of massages, from Swedish and deep tissue to aromatherapy and hot stone massages. Rejuvenate your skin with facials tailored to your needs or seek relief from muscle tension with targeted reflexology sessions. Many ships, like Scenic Luxury Cruises & Tours https://www.scenic.com.au/ and Emerald Cruises https://www.emeraldcruise s.com/river-cruises, even offer specialized beauty treatments like manicures and pedicures. Emerge from your treatment feeling restored, revitalized, and ready to face the world with renewed confidence.

- **Location:** Treatment rooms within the spa area.
- **Atmosphere:** Serene, personalized, and pampering.
- **Typical Treatments:** Massages, facials, reflexology, body wraps, beauty treatments (on some ships).
- **Fees:** Spa treatments are not included in the fare and come at an additional cost. Prices vary depending on the type and duration of the treatment.
- **Examples:** Scenic Luxury Cruises & Tours, Emerald Cruises, Uniworld Boutique River Cruises https://www.uniworld.com/

3. Move Your Body, Revive Your Soul: Fitness and Wellness Activities

Balance indulgence with invigorating activities designed to strengthen your body and uplift your spirit. Many ships offer yoga classes on the sun deck, allowing you to greet the day with mindful stretches amidst breathtaking river views. Some, like A-ROSA River Cruises https://www.a-rosa.de/flus skreuzfahrten.html and River Line https://www.rivercruise-line.eu/, also boast well-equipped gyms with cardio machines and free weights, perfect for maintaining your exercise routine while on vacation. Additionally, some cruise lines offer onboard walking groups or hiking excursions, allowing you to explore charming towns and picturesque landscapes while staying active.

- **Location:** Dedicated fitness center, sun deck, outdoor areas.
- **Atmosphere:** Energetic, motivating, and social.
- **Typical Activities:** Yoga classes, gym workouts, walking groups, hiking excursions (on some ships).
- **Included in Fare:** Fitness center access and basic yoga classes are usually included. Some specialized classes or excursions may have additional fees

4. Find Your Inner Balance: Mind-Body Therapies

Go beyond the physical and embark on a journey of inner restoration. Some ships, like Crystal River Cruises https://www.crystalcruises.com/, offer meditation sessions guided by experienced instructors, allowing you to find stillness and tranquility amidst the vibrant itinerary. Additionally, some lines offer workshops on topics like mindfulness and stress management, equipping you with tools to cultivate inner peace and well-being throughout your travels and beyond your cruise. Whether it's a guided meditation session on the sundeck as the sun dips below the horizon, a tai chi class on the riverside promenade, or a soothing aromatherapy sleep ritual in your cabin, these mind-body therapies offer a chance to reconnect with your inner self and cultivate a sense of peace that transcends the journey.

- **Location:** Dedicated spaces like meditation rooms, sun deck, cabins (for sleep rituals).
- **Atmosphere:** Calm, introspective, and restorative.
- **Typical Activities:** Meditation sessions, tai chi classes, aromatherapy workshops, sleep rituals.
- **Fees:** Some specialized workshops or private sessions may have additional fees, while basic offerings like meditation sessions are often included.

5. Beyond the Ship: Local Wellness Experiences

Enhance your onboard wellness journey by venturing ashore. Explore charming towns with farmers' markets brimming with fresh, local produce, perfect for picking up ingredients for a healthy onboard picnic. Discover quaint spas or wellness centers offering unique treatments like traditional herbal baths or rejuvenating massages with regional ingredients. Some shore excursions even incorporate visits to vineyards or breweries, allowing you to experience local wellness traditions firsthand.

- **Location:** Various charming towns and villages along the Rhine.
- **Atmosphere:** Immersive, authentic, and enriching.
- **Typical Experiences:** Farmers' markets, local spas, wellness centers, visits to vineyards or breweries.
- **Fees:** Fees vary depending on the specific activity or excursion chosen.

Tips for Making the Most of Your Cruise Experience

Maximize your Rhine River cruise with insider tips for an unforgettable journey. Optimize your time ashore, savor local flavors, and embrace cultural excursions. Engage with onboard activities, leverage amenities, and connect with fellow travelers. Enhance your cruise experience with savvy strategies tailored to enrich your exploration along the picturesque Rhine.

1. Pack Wisely, Sail Freely:

Embrace the freedom of a lighter load. River cruises navigate charming towns and quaint villages, demanding nimble mobility. Pack versatile clothing that effortlessly transitions from ship to shore, layering for unpredictable weather. Prioritize comfort over fashion, opting for shoes you can walk cobblestone streets in with ease. Remember, laundry facilities are often available onboard, so pack light and embrace the thrill of spontaneous exploration.

2. Embrace the Early Bird:

Rise and shine with the Rhine! Early mornings unveil the river's magic in its purest form – mist cloaking medieval castles, dew-kissed vineyards shimmering in the dawn light, and a serene stillness before the day unfolds. Grab a coffee and settle on the sun deck, or join an early walking group to witness the towns awakening. These quiet moments offer a deeper connection to the landscape and a unique perspective on life along the river.

3. Be a Local Hero:

Step beyond the tourist bubble. Learn a few basic German phrases – "Guten Morgen," "Danke schön," and "Bitte" go a long way. Venture beyond the main squares and explore hidden alleys, discover local cafes nestled away, and strike up conversations with shopkeepers. Embrace the spirit of "Gemütlichkeit," the German art of coziness and conviviality, and watch your experience transform from sightseeing to genuine connection.

4. Master the Art of Shore Excursions:

Choose wisely, plan strategically. Shore excursions offer a kaleidoscope of adventures, from medieval castle tours to wine tastings in centuries-old cellars. Prioritize your interests, opting for excursions that ignite your passions. Research timings to avoid overlaps and maximize your time ashore. Consider venturing out independently, renting bikes for a scenic riverside peddle or joining a local cooking class for an immersive cultural experience.

5. Embrace the Unexpected:

Leave room for serendipity. Not every moment needs to be pre-planned. Wander off the beaten path, follow your curiosity, and embrace unplanned encounters. Strike up a conversation with a fellow traveler, join a spontaneous onboard game, or simply sit on the deck and let the Rhine's rhythm lull you into a state of blissful reverie. These unscripted moments often become the most cherished memories of your journey.

6. Unplug and Unwind:

Disconnect to reconnect. Put your phone away, resist the urge to constantly check emails, and immerse yourself in the present moment. Savor the conversations, the laughter, the breathtaking scenery. Listen to the gentle lapping of water against the ship, watch the clouds drift by, and reconnect with the simple joy of being present. This digital detox will amplify your experience and leave you feeling truly rejuvenated.

7. Savor the Culinary Symphony:

Your taste buds are in for a treat. Rhine River cruises offer a delectable journey through regional specialties and international culinary delights. Don't just stick to the main dining room. Explore the cafes onboard, indulge in afternoon tea, and venture ashore to sample local delicacies in charming village restaurants. Embrace the opportunity to expand your palate and create lasting memories that revolve around shared meals and laughter.

8. Become a Night Owl:

The Rhine unfurls a different kind of magic after dark. As twilight paints the sky, enjoy a cocktail on the open deck, sharing stories and stargazing with newfound friends. Attend live music performances or participate in onboard casino nights. Some ships even offer moonlight kayaking excursions or wine tastings under the starry sky. Embrace the nocturnal energy and create memories that shimmer long after the last rays of sunshine fade.

9. Capture the Essence, Not Just the Image:

Take photographs, but also collect moments. While capturing scenic vistas and charming villages is tempting, don't let your lens become a barrier to experience. Put the camera down, breathe in the fresh air, listen to the sounds of the river, and let the emotions wash over you. These intangible memories will paint a far richer picture in your mind's eye than any photograph ever could.

10. Bid Farewell with a Grateful Heart:

As your journey draws to a close, let gratitude be your compass. Savor the final moments, take one last stroll on the sun deck, and bid farewell to your floating home with a grateful heart. Reflect on the adventures, the laughter, the connections made, and the beauty witnessed. Leave a piece of your heart on the Rhine, knowing that the magic you experienced will always be a part of you.

11. Share the Bounty, Spread the Joy:

Embrace the spirit of giving and leave a positive impact. Purchase local handicrafts from artisans selling along the riverbanks, supporting their livelihood and preserving traditional artistry. Leave a heartfelt note of appreciation for the exceptional service provided by the crew, acknowledging their contribution to your journey. Consider volunteering at a local community project during a shore excursion, making a meaningful difference and experiencing the warmth of European hospitality firsthand.

12. Learn, Listen, Grow:

Your Rhine River cruise isn't just a vacation; it's an opportunity to grow. Listen to the stories of fellow travelers, engage in conversations with locals, and immerse yourself in the rich history and culture of the regions you visit. Attend onboard lectures by guest speakers, soaking up knowledge about art, architecture, and local traditions. Be open to new perspectives, challenge your preconceptions, and return home with a broadened worldview and a deeper understanding of the world around you.

13. Embrace the Rhythm, Find Your Flow:

Don't try to pack every minute with activity. The magic of the Rhine unfolds best when embraced with a sense of ease and flow. Let the gentle rhythm of the river guide your pace. Alternate days of bustling shore excursions with tranquil moments on the deck, reading a book, or simply watching the world go by. When your body tells you to rest, pay attention to it. Remember, your vacation is not a race; it's a dance with the Rhine, and the most graceful steps are often taken at a leisurely pace.

14. Leave No Trace, Take Only Memories:

Be a responsible traveler, mindful of your impact on the environment and local communities. Dispose of waste responsibly, avoid littering, and respect the cultural norms of the regions you visit. Choose sustainable tours and excursions that support local economies and minimize environmental impact. Leave the places you visit as pristine as you found them, ensuring future travelers can enjoy their magic as well.

15. Let the Rhine River Unfold:

Ultimately, the greatest tip is to surrender to the magic of the Rhine. This enchanting river has a way of weaving its spell, revealing its secrets to those who approach it with an open heart and a curious mind. Trust the journey, embrace the unexpected, and let the Rhine River guide you on an unforgettable odyssey that will leave you forever changed.

With these tips as your compass, navigate your Rhine River cruise with confidence and delight. Remember, the journey is not just about the destinations, but about the experiences you have along the way. Embrace every moment, big and small, and prepare to be captivated by the magic of the Rhine.

Chapter 6: Shore Excursions and Activities

E nrich your Rhine River Cruise with captivating shore excursions and activities. Immerse yourself in history with museum visits, embark on adventurous experiences, and participate in cultural workshops. From exploring historical sites to engaging in hands-on demonstrations, each shore activity enhances your journey, creating lasting memories along the scenic Rhine.

Museums and Historical Sites Visits

Visit museums and historical attractions to enhance your Rhine River excursion. Discover the region's rich history by visiting old castles, fascinating museums, and cultural sites. Immerse yourself in centuries-old stories, art, and relics that weave a fascinating tapestry of history along the scenic Rhine.

1. Cologne Chocolate Museum (Schokoladenmuseum)

Step into Willy Wonka's wonderland at the Cologne Chocolate Museum. This chocoholic's dream isn't just about indulging (though there's plenty of that!). It's a fascinating journey through the history of chocolate, from its Mayan origins to modern-day decadence.

Location: Schokoladenmuseum, Im Schokoladenmuseum 1-2, 50678 Köln, Germany

Website: https://www.schokoladenmuseum.de/?lang=en

- **Historical background:** Trace the evolution of chocolate, from a sacred Aztec beverage to a global phenomenon, through interactive exhibits, historical artifacts, and live chocolate-making demonstrations.
- **Curiosity:** Witness the world's largest chocolate fountain, a cascading 15-meter river of pure cocoa bliss.
- **Practical information:** Open daily, with guided tours and self-guided exploration options available.
- **What to do and see:** Learn about the history and production of chocolate, indulge in tastings, create your own personalized chocolate bar, and witness live demonstrations of chocolate-making magic.
- **Outdoor advice:** Wear comfortable shoes for exploring the museum and surrounding Cologne Old Town.
- **Entrance fee:** €12 (adults), €6 (children)
- **Helpful tip:** Combine your visit with a stroll through Cologne's Old Town and a stop at the iconic Kölner Dom cathedral.
- **How to get there:** Easily accessible by train, plane, or car. The museum is a short walk from the main train station.

2. Gutenberg Museum (Gutenberg-Museum)

In Mainz, step back to the dawn of the printing revolution at the Gutenberg Museum. Immerse yourself in the world of Johannes Gutenberg, the inventor of the movable type printing press, and witness the transformative power of the written word.

Location: Gutenberg-Museum, Liebfrauenplatz 5, 55116 Mainz, Germany

Website: https://www.mainz.de/microsite/gutenberg-museum-en/index.php

- **Historical background:** The museum houses the Gutenberg Bible, one of the first printed books ever made, and showcases printing presses, typefaces, and other historical artifacts.

- **Curiosity:** Gutenberg's revolutionary invention democratized knowledge and laid the foundation for modern mass communication.
- **Practical information:** Open daily, with guided tours and self-guided exploration options available.
- **What to do and see:** Explore the history of printing, witness demonstrations of printing with a Gutenberg press, admire the Gutenberg Bible, and discover the impact of printing on society.
- **Outdoor advice:** Wear comfortable shoes for exploring the museum and charming Mainz Old Town.
- **Entrance fee:** €8 (adults), €4 (children)
- **Helpful tip:** Time your visit to coincide with the Gutenberg Festival in July for a vibrant celebration of printing and its legacy.
- **How to get there:** Easily accessible by train or car. The museum is located in the heart of Mainz Old Town.

3. Eltz Castle (Burg Eltz)

Perched on a rocky crag amidst lush greenery, Eltz Castle is a fairytale come to life. This 12th-century marvel, untouched by wars, offers a glimpse into medieval life and architecture.

Location: Burg Eltz 67, 56281 Wierschem, Germany

Website: https://en.wikipedia.org/wiki/Eltz_Castle

- **Historical background:** Built by the Eltz family, the castle passed down through generations and remains privately owned to this day.
- **Curiosity:** The castle's secluded location and intricate architecture, with its gabled towers and colorful facades, have inspired countless artists and writers.
- **Practical information:** Accessible by shuttle bus from the village of

Wierschem or by a scenic hike through the forest. Guided tours are available.

- **What to do and see:** Explore the castle's interior, admire the grand halls, knights' chambers, and armory, and soak in the breathtaking views of the surrounding valley.
- **Outdoor advice:** Wear sturdy shoes for the hike or shuttle bus ride and be prepared for crowds during peak season.
- **Entrance fee:** €12.50 (adults), €8 (children)
- Helpful tip: Combine your visit to Eltz Castle with a hike in the surrounding hills for an immersive experience of the Mosel Valley's natural beauty.
- **How to get there:** Train to Cochem or Bullay, followed by a bus or taxi to Wierschem.

4. Rüdesheim am Rhein

This charming town on the east bank of the Rhine isn't just about quaint streets and Riesling wine. Its Drosselgasse, a narrow alley lined with half-timbered houses, was once a bustling center for merchants and artisans.

Location: Rüdesheim am Rhein, Germany

Website: https://www.ruedesheim.de/: https://www.ruedesheim.de/

- **Historical background:** The Drosselgasse, dating back to the 14th century, reflects the prosperity of Rüdesheim's medieval past, with each house boasting unique carvings and architectural details.
- **Curiosity:** The name "Drosselgasse" translates to "Thrush Alley," possibly referencing the songbirds that once frequented the narrow lane.
- **Practical information:** Easily accessible by train, boat, or car. Explore the Drosselgasse on foot, visit the Siegfried Mechanical Music Museum, or take a boat cruise on the Rhine.
- **What to do and see:** Stroll through the Drosselgasse, marvel at the intricate carvings and colorful facades, browse local shops and artisans'

stalls, and stop for a glass of Riesling in one of the historic wine cellars.

- **Outdoor advice:** Wear comfortable shoes for walking and be prepared for crowds during peak season.
- **Entrance fee:** Free (Drosselgasse)
- **Helpful tip:** Visit Rüdesheim during the Rüdesheimer Weinfest (September) for a lively celebration of wine and local culture.
- **How to get there:** Train stations and boat piers are located in Rüdesheim.

5. Marksburg Castle

This impregnable hilltop fortress above Braubach stands as a testament to medieval ingenuity and resilience. Unlike many Rhine castles, it has never been conquered, offering a fascinating glimpse into its defensive architecture and military history.

Location: Marksburg 1, 56322 Braubach, Germany

Website: https://www.marksburg.de/: https://www.marksburg.de/

- **Historical background:** Constructed in the 13th century, Marksburg served as a refuge for royalty and a military stronghold for centuries. Its thick walls, cunningly designed gates, and strategically placed cannons ensured its impregnability.
- **Curiosity:** The castle's ingenious water supply system, utilizing rainwater stored in cisterns, allowed inhabitants to withstand long sieges.
- **Practical information:** Open daily, with guided tours and self-guided exploration options available.
- **What to do and see:** Explore the castle's interior, discover its defensive mechanisms, learn about its military history, and walk the ramparts for stunning views of the Rhine Gorge.
- **Outdoor advice:** Wear comfortable shoes for climbing uphill and be prepared for crowds during peak season.
- **Entrance fee:** €12 (adults), €6 (children)

- **Helpful tip:** Combine your visit to Marksburg with a boat cruise on the Rhine for a full experience of the gorge's beauty.
- **How to get there:** Marksburg is accessible by car or bus from Braubach. A short hike from the village leads to the castle.

Bonus tip: Consider purchasing a Rhine Pass for discounted travel on trains and boats throughout the region, maximizing your exploration and saving money.

Active and Adventurous Shore Activities

Unleash adventure along the Rhine River with a spectrum of active shore activities. Explore cycling trails tracing historic towns, indulge in vineyard hikes, or opt for kayaking along picturesque stretches. From castle tours to culinary explorations, elevate your Rhine experience with thrilling and immersive onshore adventures.

1. Conquer the Rhine Valley Cycle Path (Various Locations)

- **Location:** The entire Rhine Valley, with designated sections near major ports like Cologne, Mainz, and Rüdesheim.
- **Best Time:** Spring (March-May) or Autumn (September-November) for mild weather.

Imagine pedaling through vineyards, quaint villages, and past majestic castles, all while the Rhine whispers its secrets beside you. The Rhine Valley Cycle Path, a 310km ribbon of asphalt, offers breathtaking scenery and varying difficulty levels. Choose a section near your port, rent a bike, and let the wind guide you.

- **Website:** https://en.eurovelo.com/ev15
- **Fee:** Bike rentals vary, expect around €15-20 per day.
- **What to Bring:** Comfortable clothing, helmet, sunscreen, water bottle, and a sense of adventure.

- **Tip:** Pack a picnic lunch and stop at a charming village for a riverside feast.

2. Kayak the Lorelei's Echo Chamber (Near St. Goar)

- **Location:** Lorelei Felsen, near St. Goar, Germany.
- **Best Time:** Summer (June–August) for warmer water, but be prepared for crowds.

Channel your inner Rhine nymph and paddle through the Lorelei's legendary echo chamber. Glide past the towering rock face where the siren's song lured sailors to their doom, and test the acoustics yourself, your cries will bounce back in an eerie, mesmerizing melody.

- **Website:** https://en.wikipedia.org/wiki/Lorelei
- **Fee:** Kayak rentals and guided tours available, expect around €20–30 per person.
- **What to Bring:** Life jacket, swimwear, sunscreen, and a waterproof camera.
- **Tip:** Go early to avoid crowds and kayak against the current for a smoother ride.

3. Hike the Drachenfels (Near Königswinter)

- **Location:** Drachenfels, Königswinter, Germany.
- **Best Time:** Spring or autumn for comfortable hiking temperatures and stunning foliage.

Lace up your boots and conquer the Drachenfels, a rugged peak overlooking the Rhine. This moderate 4km trail winds through forests and vineyards, culminating in breathtaking panoramic views of the river valley. Reward yourself with a stein of local beer at the historic Drachenfels Castle perched on the summit.

- **Website:** https://www.schloss-drachenburg.de/index.php/de/
- **Fee:** Free to hike, castle entrance fee applies.
- **What to Bring:** Sturdy shoes, hiking poles (optional), water bottle, and camera.
- **Tip:** Pack a snack for the summit, and don't miss the breathtaking sunrise views.

4. Spelunking in the Erdbach Caves (Near Rüdesheim)

- **Location:** Erdbach Caves, near Rüdesheim, Germany.
- **Best Time:** Year-round, cave temperature is a constant 10°C.

Descend into the mysterious underworld of the Erdbach Caves, a labyrinthine network of tunnels carved by the Erbach River. Guided tours lead you through stalagmites and stalactites sculpted into fantastical shapes, past underground waterfalls, and into hidden chambers echoing with the river's flow. It's an adventure for all ages and a glimpse into the Earth's hidden secrets.

- **Website:** https://de.wikipedia.org/wiki/Erdbachh%C3%B6hle
- **Fee:** Guided tour fees apply, expect around €10-15 per person.
- **What to Bring:** Warm clothing, comfortable shoes, and a sense of wonder.
- **Tip:** Wear clothes you don't mind getting dirty and be prepared for some low ceilings and narrow passages.

5. Zipline Through the Trees (Near Rüdesheim)

- **Location:** Adlerwald Forest, near Rüdesheim, Germany.
- **Best Time:** Spring or summer for lush foliage and comfortable temperatures.

Feel the wind whip through your hair as you soar through the treetops on the exhilarating zipline course in the Adlerwald Forest. Glide from platform to platform, weaving through the canopy and enjoying bird's-eye views of the

Rhine Valley below. Different levels of difficulty cater to all thrill-seekers, from gentle glides to adrenaline-pumping descents.

- **Website:** https://www.niederwalddenkmal.de/rund-um-das-niederwald denkmal/ruedesheimer-adlerwarte/
- **Fee:** Varies depending on the chosen course, expect around €20-40 per person.
- **What to Bring:** Comfortable clothing and shoes, sunscreen, and a sense of adventure.
- **Tip:** Book your zipline experience in advance, especially during peak season.

6. Canyoning in the Black Forest (Near Freiburg)

- **Location:** Triberg Waterfalls, Black Forest, Germany.
- **Best Time:** Spring (May-June) or autumn (September-October) for optimal water levels.

Embark on an aquatic adventure through the heart of the Black Forest. Canyoning tours take you down cascading waterfalls, through moss-covered gorges, and across natural rockslides. Rappel down sheer rock faces, plunge into crystal-clear pools, and conquer your fear of heights in this exhilarating experience.

- **Website:** https://en.wikipedia.org/wiki/Triberg_Waterfalls
- **Fee:** Guided tour fees apply, expect around €50-80 per person.
- **What to Bring:** Swimwear, wetsuit (optional), waterproof shoes, helmet, and a sense of daring.
- **Tip:** Choose a tour that matches your fitness level and experience and be prepared for some cold water!

7. Paraglide Over the Rhine Gorge (Near Boppard)

- **Location:** Boppard, Germany.
- **Best Time:** Spring or summer for calm weather conditions.

Take to the skies and experience the breathtaking beauty of the Rhine Gorge from a bird's-eye view. Tandem paragliding flights allow you to soar alongside an experienced pilot, effortlessly gliding over the winding river, lush vineyards, and ancient castles. Feel the wind beneath your wings and witness the panoramic splendor of the Rhine Valley unfold before you.

- **Website:** https://www.bellevue-boppard.de/paragliding
- **Fee:** Tandem flight fees apply, expect around €100-150 per person.
- **What to Bring:** Comfortable clothing and shoes, sunglasses, and a sense of wonder.
- **Tip:** Book your paragliding flight in advance, especially during peak season. Consider your comfort level with heights and discuss any concerns with your pilot before takeoff.

Cultural Workshops and Demonstrations

Take part in fascinating cultural workshops and demonstrations to fully immerse yourself in the cultural tapestry of the Rhine. Discover the history of the area through interactive activities like wine tastings and artisanal crafts. Enjoy engaging discussions that provide a deeper understanding of regional customs and the diversity of cultures along this historic river.

1. Craft Your Own Cuckoo Clock in Triberg

- **Location:** Triberg, Germany. Schwarzwaldmuseum Triberg, Hauptstraße 39, 78166 Triberg.
- **Best Time:** Year-round.

Step into the heart of cuckoo clock country and learn the intricate art of crafting these iconic timepieces. The Schwarzwaldmuseum offers workshops where you can assemble your own miniature cuckoo clock, guided by skilled artisans. From selecting wood pieces to painting delicate details, feel the rhythm of the forest come alive in your hands.

- **Website:** https://www.triberg.de/tourismus-freizeit/tourismus-freizeit/ sehens-und-erlebenswertes/schwarzwaldmuseum-sehen-hoeren-staunen
- **Fee:** Varies depending on the chosen workshop, expect around €15-30 per person.
- **What to Bring:** Comfortable clothing, a curious mind, and a steady hand.
- **Tip:** Book your workshop in advance, especially during peak season. Don't be afraid to ask questions and embrace the meticulous process.

2. Master the Art of Pretzel Baking in Heidelberg

- **Location:** Heidelberg, Germany. Bäckerei und Café Gundel, Hauptstraße 119, 69117 Heidelberg.
- **Best Time:** Fridays (9:30 AM - 12:30 PM).

Unleash your inner baker and learn the secrets of pretzel perfection at Bäckerei und Café Gundel. This family-run bakery offers weekly workshops where you'll knead, twist, and sprinkle your way to golden-brown bliss. Master the traditional "Laugenbrezel" or get creative with sweet variations. As the aroma of freshly baked pretzels fills the air, savor the warmth of German hospitality and indulge in your handiwork.

- **Website:** https://www.gundel-heidelberg.de/
- **Fee:** €25 per person, including ingredients and refreshments.
- **What to Bring:** An apron, enthusiasm, and an empty stomach!
- **Tip:** Arrive early to secure a spot, and wear comfortable clothes you can move around in. Don't hesitate to ask the bakers for tips – they're passionate about sharing their craft.

3. Unravel the Magic of Mosel Winemaking in Cochem

· **Location:** Cochem, Germany. Weingut Markus Molitor, Moselweinstraße 3, 56814 Cochem.
· **Best Time:** September-October during harvest season.

Immerse yourself in the world-renowned viticulture of the Mosel Valley. Weingut Markus Molitor, a family-owned winery nestled amidst rolling vineyards, offers interactive workshops where you can learn about grape varietals, traditional winemaking techniques, and even participate in the harvest itself. Feel the sun-warmed grapes in your hands, discover the secrets of fermentation, and savor the fruits (or grapes, rather!) of your labor.

· **Website:** https://www.markusmolitor.com/
· **Fee:** Varies depending on the chosen workshop, expect around €20-50 per person.
· **What to Bring:** Sturdy shoes for potential vineyard walks, comfortable clothing, and a thirst for knowledge (and wine!).
· **Tip:** Wear weather-appropriate clothing, as workshops might involve outdoor activities. Book your spot in advance, especially during harvest season.

4. Dance to the Rhythm of the Lorelei in Rüdesheim

· **Location:** Rüdesheim, Germany. Rüdesheimer Winzerverein, Rheinstraße 51, 65385 Rüdesheim am Rhein.
· **Best Time:** Wednesdays (8:00 PM - 10:00 PM).

Let the spirit of the Rhine guide your feet in a traditional German folk dance workshop. The Rüdesheimer Winzerverein hosts weekly sessions where you can learn the lively steps of the "Rheinländer" or the graceful waltz. No prior experience is necessary, just a willingness to embrace the joyful spirit of these time-honored dances. As you spin and twirl amidst fellow travelers and locals, connect with the vibrant culture of the region and create memories that move to the rhythm of the river.

- **Website:** https://www.weinbauverein-thuengersheim.de/
- **Fee:** Free entry, donations welcome.
- **What to Bring:** Comfortable shoes, loose clothing, and a smile!
- **Tip:** Arrive early to secure a spot, and don't be shy – locals love to welcome newcomers to the dance floor.

5. Embark on a Medieval Manuscript Journey in Cologne

- **Location:** Cologne, Germany. Museum Schnütgen, Unter Sachsenhausen 1, 50667 Köln.
- **Best Time:** Year-round.

Step back in time and delve into the intricate world of medieval illumination at the Museum Schnütgen. This renowned museum offers unique workshops where you can learn the art of calligraphy, manuscript painting, and gold leafing. Under the guidance of expert instructors, experiment with quill pens, vibrant pigments, and delicate brushstrokes. Create your own miniature masterpiece or embellish a pre-printed design, channeling the creativity of medieval scribes and monks.

- **Website:** https://www.museum-schnuetgen.de/
- **Fee:** Vary depending on the chosen workshop, expect around €15-40 per person.
- **What to Bring:** An open mind, steady hands, and a sense of awe for the beauty of ancient artistry.
- **Tip:** Pre-booking is recommended, especially during peak season. Wear comfortable clothing and be prepared for focused work (but rewarded by stunning results!).

Chapter 7: Captivating Culture Along the Rhine

T ake in the vibrant cultural tapestry that borders the Rhine River. Enjoy regional customs, sample the best cuisine in river ports, and partake in wine tastings and culinary treats. Let the Rhine's fascinating culture reveal itself, from distinctive rituals to gastronomic festivals, and make moments treasured by this picturesque river.

Local Traditions and Customs

Your Rhine River cruise promises not just fairytale castles and verdant vineyards, but also a vibrant tapestry of traditions woven into the fabric of each charming town and bustling city. From festive celebrations to quirky customs, immersing yourself in these local practices deepens your connection to the region and creates memories that transcend mere sightseeing.

1. Festive Revelry:

Step into a world of vibrant celebrations. Throughout the year, towns along the Rhine come alive with joyous festivals. Witness the vibrant costumes and lively music of Carnival in Cologne, or lose yourself in the twinkling lights and Christmas markets of Rüdesheim. Join the revelry of the Heidelberg Wine Festival, where laughter mingles with the aroma of freshly pressed grapes.

Remember, these celebrations are not just for spectators, but invitations to participate. Don your lederhosen at Oktoberfest, sway to the rhythm of a local folk dance, and discover the joy of shared traditions.

2. Culinary Delights:

Savor the flavors of tradition. Each region along the Rhine boasts its own culinary treasures, passed down through generations. Sample hearty Spätzle noodles in Swabia, indulge in fragrant Flammkuchen flatbread in Alsace, or savor a juicy Rheinschinken (Rhine ham) in Cologne. Don't shy away from local delicacies like Blutwurst (blood sausage) or Sauerkraut – they might surprise you with their hidden depths of flavor. Remember, food is a window into a culture, so embrace the unfamiliar and let your taste buds become ambassadors of cultural understanding.

3. The River's Rhythm:

The Rhine is not just a waterway, but a living heartbeat. Witness the ancient tradition of "Rheinbewohner," families who have lived and worked on the river for generations. Watch as skilled boatmen navigate the currents with practiced ease, and listen to the rhythmic lapping of water against the ship's hull. Embark on a wine cruise, gliding past sun-drenched vineyards, or join a local fishing expedition, casting your line and connecting with the river's bounty. The Rhine's rhythm is an invitation to slow down, appreciate the simple pleasures, and reconnect with the natural world.

4. Echoes of History:

Medieval castles whisper tales of chivalry, charming villages hold secrets of forgotten artisans, and vibrant cities bear witness to centuries of cultural exchange. Immerse yourself in the Rhine's rich history. Visit the majestic Cologne Cathedral, a masterpiece of Gothic architecture, or explore the haunting ruins of Eltz Castle, perched atop a rocky crag. Delve into the vibrant folklore of the region, where gnomes and fairies dance in moonlit forests, and discover the stories etched into the very stones of these ancient towns.

5. A Warm Welcome:

The Rhine people are renowned for their hospitality. Don't be surprised by a friendly "Guten Tag" or a helping hand offered with a genuine smile. Engage in conversation, ask questions about local customs, and learn a few basic German phrases. The warmth of the people is as much a part of the region's charm as its scenic landscapes. Embrace their open hearts and let yourself be welcomed into their community, even for a fleeting moment.

Remember, experiencing local traditions is not about ticking boxes on a checklist. It's about immersing yourself in the spirit of the place, showing respect for their customs, and embracing the unexpected. Wander down cobblestone streets, savor the aroma of freshly baked bread from a local bakery, or strike up a conversation with a shopkeeper. The most authentic experiences often happen when you least expect them, so keep your eyes open, and your heart open, and be prepared to be surprised.

Local Cuisine Highlights in River Cruise Ports

Cologne, Germany

Frühstückbuffet at Früh am Dom: Fuel your explorations with a hearty "Frühstücksbuffet" overlooking the magnificent Cologne Cathedral. Indulge in crusty bread, sliced meats, cheeses, fresh fruits, and the iconic "Kartoffelpuffer" (potato pancakes). (€10-15)

- **Address:** Unter Taschenmacher 3, 50667 Köln, Germany
- **Website:** https://www.frueh-am-dom.de/

Schnitzel at Peters Schnitzelstube: Dive into a colossal "Schnitzel" with creamy mashed potatoes and tangy sauerkraut at this traditional "Schnitzel-haus." Wash it down with a refreshing "Kölsch" beer, Cologne's local brew. (€15-20)

- **Address:** Große Neugasse 2-4, 50667 Köln, Germany
- **Website:** https://www.facebook.com/p/Gastst%C3%A4tte-Das-Schnitze lhaus-100054305510601/

Chocolate Dream at Schokoladenmuseum: Immerse yourself in a Willy Wonka-esque wonderland at the Schokoladenmuseum, where you can learn about chocolate's history, witness its production, and even create your own pralines. (€8-12)

- **Address:** Am Schokoladenmuseum 1, 50678 Köln, Germany
- **Website:** https://www.schokoladenmuseum.de/?lang=en

Amsterdam, Netherlands

Stroopwafel on the go: These thin waffle cookies, sandwiched with a gooey caramel filling, are a Dutch classic. Grab a warm one from a street vendor like Stroopwafelshop Van Rijn or Albert Heijn supermarkets and savor its sweet, gooey goodness. (€1-2)

- **Stroopwafelshop Van Rijn:** Address: De Dam 18, 1012 NP Amsterdam, Netherlands
- **Albert Heijn supermarkets:** Various locations throughout Amsterdam

Pannenkoeken at De Pannekoekenbakker: Treat yourself to a savory "Pan-nenkoek" topped with bacon, cheese, and onions at this cozy restaurant with a charming atmosphere. Don't miss their sweet options like apple and cinnamon or Nutella and banana. (€10-15)

- **Address:** Singel 406, 1012 AB Amsterdam, Netherlands

- **Website:** https://www.pannekoekenbakker.nl/

Rijsttafel at Restaurant Oasis: Experience the Indonesian feast of "Rijsttafel," featuring an array of small dishes like spicy satay skewers, fragrant curries, and fresh vegetables. Try Restaurant Oasis for its authentic flavors and generous portions. (€20-25)

- **Address:** Voetboogstraat 11, 1012 VB Amsterdam, Netherlands
- **Website:** https://www.tripadvisor.nl/Restaurant_Review-g1723175-d163 6477-Reviews-Oasis_restaurant-Oyster_Pond_Sint_Maarten_St_Mar tin_St_Maarten.html

Rüdesheim am Rhein, Germany

Rüdesheimer Kaffee at a terrace cafe: Savor the strong, sweet "Rüdesheimer Kaffee" flavored with Asbach brandy and topped with whipped cream while soaking in the panoramic views of the Rhine Valley. Enjoy it at a cafe like Rheingau Terrasse or Cafe & Konditorei Lindenhof. (€5-7)

- **Rheingau Terrasse:** Address: Rheinstraße 29, 65385 Rüdesheim am Rhein, Germany
- **Cafe & Konditorei Lindenhof:** Address: Drosselgasse 10, 65385 Rüdesheim am Rhein, Germany

Weinwanderung through the vineyards: Hike through the picturesque vineyards and sample different Riesling wines at charming wineries like Weingut Georg Breuer or Weingut Robert Weil. Learn about the winemaking process and discover the unique terroir of the region. (€10-15 per tasting)

- **Weingut Georg Breuer:** Address: Niederbergstraße 109, 65385 Rüdesheim am Rhein, Germany
- **Weingut Robert Weil:** Address: Rheingauer Straße 110-112, 65385 Rüdesheim am Rhein, Germany

Ritteressen at Restaurant Zum Ritter

Travel back in time at Restaurant Zum Ritter, where you'll be transported to a medieval feast fit for a king. Dressed in period costumes, waitstaff serve hearty dishes like:

- Gebratenes Spanferkel (roasted suckling pig): The star of the show, this tender and flavorful dish is cooked to crispy perfection.
- Hirschgulasch mit Rotkohl und Knödeln (deer goulash with red cabbage and dumplings): A hearty stew simmered in red wine and spices, served with fluffy potato dumplings.
- Flammkuchen mit Speck und Zwiebeln (onion and bacon tart): A thin, crispy dough topped with savory toppings, perfect for sharing.
- Gemüseauflauf (vegetable gratin): A creamy and comforting side dish featuring seasonal vegetables.

No feast is complete without libations, so raise a tankard of:

- Met (honey mead): A sweet and heady drink, enjoyed by knights and commoners alike.
- Dunkles Bier (dark beer): A rich and malty brew, perfect for washing down the hearty meal.
- Rheinwein (Rhine wine): Sample the region's famous Riesling or Spätburgunder with your meal.

Immerse yourself in the experience:

- Live medieval music and performances add to the atmosphere.
- Participate in traditional games and activities like axe throwing or arm wrestling.
- Feast with your hands, just like they did in the Middle Ages!

Practicalities:

- **Address:** Drosselgasse 1, 65385 Rüdesheim am Rhein, Germany
- **Website:** https://www.tripadvisor.dk/Hotel_Review-g12802522-d12706 252-Reviews-Landgasthof_Ritter-Herzogenweiler_Baden_Wurttember g.html
- **Price:** €30-40 per person, depending on the menu chosen.
- **Reservations recommended:** This popular restaurant can fill up quickly, especially during peak season.

Wine Tasting and Culinary Experiences

Wine Tastings:

Rüdesheim am Rhein, Germany:

Weingut Georg Breuer: Nestled amid the sun-drenched vineyards, this esteemed winery offers an immersive experience. Learn about Riesling production from vine to glass, then swirl, sniff, and sip their award-winning wines. (€15-25 per tasting)

- **Address:** Niederbergstraße 109, 65385 Rüdesheim am Rhein, Germany
- **Website:** http://georg-breuer.com/weine/

Kloster Eberbach: Step back in time at this historic abbey, transformed into a renowned winery. Explore the medieval cellars, then indulge in a guided tasting featuring Rieslings that express the unique terroir of the Rheingau region. (€20-30 per tasting)

- **Address:** Kloster Eberbach, 65375 Oestrich-Winkel, Germany
- **Website:** https://kloster-eberbach.de/en

Cochem, Germany:

Weingut Reichsgraf von Kesselstatt: Perched high above the Mosel River, this picturesque winery boasts breathtaking views and exquisite wines. Savor their Mosel Rieslings, known for their delicate minerality and fruit-forward character. (€10-20 per tasting)

- **Address:** Schloßstraße 57, 56814 Cochem, Germany
- **Website:** https://www.kesselstatt.de/

Weingut Balthasar Ress: This family-run winery champions sustainable practices and produces biodynamic Mosel Rieslings that express the terroir's vibrant personality. Enjoy a guided tasting in their charming tasting room or on their panoramic terrace. (€15-25 per tasting)

- **Address:** Balduinstraße 14, 56814 Cochem, Germany
- **Website:** https://www.balthasar-ress.de/

Culinary Experiences:

Colmar, France:

La Maison des Têtes Couronnées: Immerse yourself in Alsatian gastronomy at this historic restaurant housed in a 16th-century building. Indulge in traditional dishes like "choucroute garnie" (sauerkraut with sausages) or "flammekueche" (Alsatian tart) paired with local wines. (€25-40 per person)

- **Address:** 7 Place de l'Ancienne Douane, 68000 Colmar, France
- **Website:** https://www.maisondestetes.com/en/

Alsace Cooking Class: Get hands-on and learn the secrets of Alsatian cuisine at a local cooking class. Master the art of making "spätzle" (egg noodles), prepare a flavorful coq au vin, and finish with a decadent tarte flambée. (€50-70 per person)

- **Cook'n Joy:** Rue des Marchands 36, 68000 Colmar, France
- **L'Atelier du Cuisinier:** Rue des Clefs 13, 68000 Colmar, France

Heidelberg, Germany:

Marktplatz Food Tour: Wander through bustling Heidelberg's historic market square and explore its culinary delights. Sample local cheeses, sausages, and fresh produce, learn about regional specialties, and discover hidden gems you wouldn't find on your own. (€40-50 per person)

Heidelberg Food Tours: https://www.heidelherz.com/touren/altstadt-food-tour-heidelberg/

Heidelberger Brauerei: Craft Beer & Sausage Pairing: Get a taste of German brewing tradition at this historic brewery. Tour the facility, learn about their beer-making process, and then savor a flight of their handcrafted brews paired with locally sourced sausages and cheeses. (€15-20 per person)

- **Address:** Am Schlossgarten 2, 69120 Heidelberg, Germany
- **Website:** https://www.heidelberger-brauerei.de/: https://www.heidelberger-brauerei.de/

Beyond the Tastings and Experiences:

Remember, these are just a few suggestions to whet your appetite. Your Rhine River cruise offers a treasure trove of culinary adventures waiting to be discovered. Don't be afraid to stray from the itinerary, explore local markets, chat with vendors, and try dishes that pique your curiosity. The following are some extra tips that will enhance your experience:

- **Ask your cruise line:** Many cruises offer onboard wine tastings, cooking demonstrations, and themed dinners featuring regional specialties. Take advantage of these unique experiences.

- **Embrace local markets:** Immerse yourself in the vibrant atmosphere of local markets, sample fresh produce and artisanal products, and pick up picnic ingredients for a scenic riverside lunch.
- **Learn a few German phrases:** Saying "Bitte" (please) and "Danke" (thank you) goes a long way in building rapport with locals and enhancing your experience.
- **Be adventurous:** Don't be afraid to try something new! You might discover your new favorite dish or wine.

Culinary Events and Festivals

Enjoy the culinary delights of the Rhine River by attending one of its many gastronomy events and festivals. Immerse yourself on a savory voyage, relishing the rich traditions and different cuisines that beautify this gorgeous canal, from wine tastings along the vineyard-lined banks to food fairs showcasing local delicacies.

1. Rüdesheim Wine Festival (September)

- **Venue:** Rüdesheim am Rhein, Germany (Heart of Rheingau wine region)
- **Dates:** September 8-17, 2024
- **Website:** https://www.ruedesheimer-weinfest.de/
- **Fees:** Free entry; food and drinks purchased à la carte

Experience: Immerse yourself in the vibrant tapestry of Rüdesheim's wine celebration. Stroll through charming stalls overflowing with local vintages, from crisp Rieslings to robust Spätburgunders. Savor regional delicacies like "Handkäs mit Musik" (pungent cheese with onions and music) and "Spundekäs" (creamy cheese with caraway seeds), all while the lively atmosphere pulsates with music and laughter.

2. Cochem Wine Festival (September)

- **Venue:** Cochem, Germany (Picturesque town along the Mosel River)
- **Dates:** September 27-30, 2024
- **Website:** https://www.ferienland-cochem.de/en/events/wine-festivals
- **Fees:** Free entry; food and drinks purchased à la carte

Experience: Step into a fairytale setting with half-timbered houses lining the streets, a majestic Reichsburg crowning the hill, and the intoxicating aroma of Riesling filling the air. The Cochem Wine Festival offers a delightful swirl of wine tastings, live music, and traditional fare like "Winzerbraten" (grilled pork) and "Dibbelchen" (potato dumplings).

3. Koblenz Wine Festival (July)

- **Venue:** Deutsches Eck, Koblenz, Germany (Convergence of the Rhine and Mosel Rivers)
- **Dates:** July 26-August 4, 2024
- **Website:** https://www.weinfestival-koblenz.de/en
- **Fees:** Free entry; food and drinks purchased à la carte

Experience: Witness the grand spectacle of the Koblenz Wine Festival, where over 100 winemakers showcase their finest creations against the backdrop of the majestic Deutsches Eck. Sip on award-winning wines from across the region, indulge in gourmet street food, and enjoy live music and entertainment on the banks of the Rhine and Mosel.

4. Mainz Cheese Market (April)

- **Venue:** Domplatz, Mainz, Germany (Historic city center)
- **Dates:** April 27-28, 2024
- **Website:** http://kaesemarktmainz.de/
- **Fees:** Free entry

Experience: Embark on a cheesy adventure at the Mainz Cheese Market.

This renowned event boasts over 200 stalls overflowing with an array of regional and international cheeses, from creamy Brie to sharp Cheddar. Meet passionate cheesemakers, savor samples, and learn about the art of cheesemaking through workshops and demonstrations.

5. Medieval Feast at Marksburg Castle (April-October)

- **Venue:** Marksburg Castle, Braubach, Germany (Hilltop castle overlooking the Rhine Gorge)
- **Dates:** April-October, various dates (check website for schedule)
- **Website:** https://www.marksburg-schaenke.de/testdrive/EN/medievalba nquet.php
- **Fees:** €59 per person (includes feast and castle tour)

Experience: Travel back in time at the Marksburg Castle's Medieval Feast. This immersive experience transports you to the 16th century with a traditional four-course meal served in the grand Knights' Hall. Savor authentic dishes like roasted boar, stews, and pastries, all accompanied by live music and storytelling.

Pro Tips:

- Book festival tickets and castle feasts in advance, especially during peak season.
- Pack comfortable shoes for exploring towns and vineyards.
- Brush up on basic German phrases; a little effort goes a long way.
- Embrace the local culture and don't be afraid to try new things!

Chapter 8: Rhine River Cruise Calendar

N avigate the enchanting Rhine River Cruise Calendar, brimming with captivating events and festivals. Explore the vibrant tapestry of local celebrations along the banks, from cultural festivals to wine tastings. Uncover the allure of 2024's special cruises and themed experiences, ensuring an immersive and unforgettable journey along this historic waterway.

Events and Festivals Along the Rhine

1. Rüdesheim Wine Festival (September)

- **Venue:** Rüdesheim am Rhein, Germany (Heart of Rheingau wine region)
- **Dates:** September 8-17, 2024
- **Website:** https://www.ruedesheimer-weinfest.de/
- **Fees:** Free entry; food and drinks purchased à la carte

Immerse yourself in the electrifying atmosphere of Rüdesheim's wine extravaganza. Stroll through charming stalls laden with local vintages, from crisp Rieslings to robust Spätburgunders. Savor regional delicacies like "Handkäs mit Musik" (pungent cheese with onions and music) and "Spundekäs" (creamy cheese with caraway seeds), all while the lively ambiance pulsates with music and laughter.

2. Cochem Wine Festival (September)

- **Venue:** Cochem, Germany (Picturesque town along the Mosel River)
- **Dates:** September 27-30, 2024
- **Website:** https://www.ferienland-cochem.de/en/events/wine-festivals
- **Fees:** Free entry; food and drinks purchased à la carte

Step into a fairytale setting with half-timbered houses lining the streets, a majestic Reichsburg crowning the hill, and the intoxicating aroma of Riesling filling the air. The Cochem Wine Festival offers a delightful swirl of wine tastings, live music, and traditional fare like "Winzerbraten" (grilled pork) and "Dibbelchen" (potato dumplings).

3. Koblenz Wine Festival (July)

- **Venue:** Deutsches Eck, Koblenz, Germany (Convergence of the Rhine and Mosel Rivers)
- **Dates:** July 26-August 4, 2024
- **Website:** https://www.weinfestival-koblenz.de/
- **Fees:** Free entry; food and drinks purchased à la carte

Witness the grand spectacle of the Koblenz Wine Festival, where over 100 winemakers showcase their finest creations against the backdrop of the majestic Deutsches Eck. Sip on award-winning wines from across the region, indulge in gourmet street food, and enjoy live music and entertainment on the banks of the Rhine and Mosel.

4. Mainz Cheese Market (April)

- **Venue:** Domplatz, Mainz, Germany (Historic city center)
- **Dates:** April 27-28, 2024
- **Website:** http://kaesemarktmainz.de/
- **Fees:** Free entry

Embark on a cheesy adventure at the Mainz Cheese Market. This renowned event boasts over 200 stalls overflowing with an array of regional and international cheeses, from creamy Brie to sharp Cheddar. Meet passionate cheesemakers, savor samples, and learn about the art of cheesemaking through workshops and demonstrations.

5. Medieval Feast at Marksburg Castle (April-October)

- **Venue:** Marksburg Castle, Braubach, Germany (Hilltop castle overlooking the Rhine Gorge)
- **Dates:** April-October, various dates (check website for schedule)
- **Website:** https://www.marksburg-schaenke.de/testdrive/EN/medievalbanquet.php
- **Fees:** €59 per person (includes feast and castle tour)

Travel back in time at the Marksburg Castle's Medieval Feast. This immersive experience transports you to the 16th century with a traditional four-course meal served in the grand Knights' Hall. Savor authentic dishes like roasted boar, stews, and pastries, all accompanied by live music and storytelling.

6. Bacharach Winegrowers' Festival (October)

- **Venue:** Bacharach, Germany (Picturesque town with half-timbered houses)
- **Dates:** October 4-6, 2024
- **Website:** https://www.bacharach.de/freizeit/veranstaltungen
- **Fees:** Free entry

Embrace the spirit of autumn in Bacharach, where the Winegrowers' Festival celebrates the region's bounty. Stroll through the historic marketplace adorned with colorful foliage, sample local vintages from the surrounding vineyards, and delight in traditional dishes like Flammkuchen (savory tart) and Zwiebelkuchen (onion tart). Live music and folk dancing add to the festive atmosphere.

7. Cologne Christmas Markets (November-December)

- **Venue:** Cologne, Germany (Major city along the Rhine)
- **Dates:** November 21 - December 23, 2024
- **Website:** https://www.koelnerweihnachtsmarkt.com/
- **Fees:** Free entry

Let the magic of Christmas engulf you at Cologne's enchanting Christmas markets. Wander through twinkling stalls brimming with handcrafted ornaments, toys, and delicious treats like gingerbread, roasted chestnuts, and glühwein (mulled wine). Embrace the warmth and cheer, soak in the festive atmosphere, and create unforgettable holiday memories.

Tips:

- Book festival tickets and castle feasts in advance, especially during peak season.
- Pack comfortable shoes for exploring towns and vineyards.
- Brush up on basic German phrases; a little effort goes a long way.
- Embrace the local culture and don't be afraid to try new things!
- Pace yourself and savor each culinary experience.
- Plan your itinerary around the events that most excite you.
- Remember to pack a reusable water bottle so you can keep hydrated.
- Consider purchasing a wine pass for discounts and tastings at multiple vineyards.

Special Cruises and Themes in 2024

In 2024, succumbed to the temptation of the Rhine River's Special Cruises and Themes. From themed cruises celebrating art, history, and gastronomic pleasures to private itineraries highlighting hidden jewels, embark on bespoke experiences along this renowned canal, delivering unforgettable moments and distinct perspectives for every traveler.

1. Wine & Wellness Cruise (August-September)

- **Cruise Line:** Viking Cruises (various departure points)
- **Website:** https://www.vikingcruises.com/
- **Fees:** Starting from €2,499 per person
- **Dates:** Various departures throughout August and September

Indulge in a holistic journey where pampering meets vintage. This cruise seamlessly blends wellness activities like yoga, meditation, and spa treatments with immersive wine experiences. Learn the art of winemaking, explore charming vineyards, and savor gourmet pairings as you cruise through picturesque landscapes.

2. Christmas Markets Cruise (December)

- **Cruise Line:** Emerald Waterways (various departure points)
- **Website:** https://www.emeraldcruises.com/
- **Fees:** Starting from €3,999 per person
- **Dates:** Various departures throughout December

Transform your Rhine River cruise into a magical winter wonderland. This festive voyage whisks you through fairytale towns adorned with twinkling lights and bustling Christmas markets. Sip on steaming mugs of glühwein, browse handcrafted ornaments, and soak in the joyous atmosphere as carolers fill the air with cheer.

3. Culinary Delights Cruise (April-May)

- **Cruise Line:** Avalon Waterways (various departure points)
- **Website:** https://www.avalonwaterways.com/
- **Fees:** Starting from €3,499 per person
- **Dates:** Various departures throughout April and May

Awaken your inner gourmand with this culinary odyssey. This cruise takes you on a gastronomic adventure, visiting Michelin-starred restaurants, local wineries, and charming cafes along the Rhine. Learn the secrets of regional specialties, participate in cooking classes, and savor the freshest seasonal produce paired with exquisite wines.

4. Active Rhine & Bike Cruise (May-September)

- **Cruise Line:** Uniworld Boutique River Cruises (various departure points)
- **Website:** https://www.uniworld.com/
- **Fees:** Starting from €2,999 per person
- **Dates:** Various departures throughout May to September

Embrace the active side of the Rhine with this bike-and-cruise adventure. Cycle through charming villages, vineyards, and scenic trails, stopping to admire medieval castles and picturesque towns along the way. Your evenings are spent relaxing aboard the luxurious ship, enjoying gourmet meals and breathtaking river views.

5. Family Fun & Adventure Cruise (July-August)

- **Cruise Line:** Scenic Cruises (various departure points)
- **Website:** https://www.scenicusa.com/river-cruises
- **Fees:** Starting from €2,799 per person
- **Dates:** Various departures throughout July and August

Turn your family vacation into an unforgettable adventure. This cruise caters to all ages, with interactive games, themed activities, and onboard entertainment designed for children. Explore castles, participate in treasure hunts, and let the kids learn about local history and culture through engaging programs.

Chapter 9: Photography Tips

The Rhine River, snaking through vine-clad hills and fairytale towns, is a painter's dream come true. But for us photography enthusiasts, it's a playground of light, color, and composition, a chance to translate its magic into timeless images. So, whether you're a seasoned pro or a smartphone-wielding adventurer, prepare to be dazzled! Here are some tips to ensure your Rhine River cruise photos sing:

Capturing Scenic Landscapes:

- **Embrace the Golden Hour:** As the sun paints the sky in hues of orange and rose, the Rhine transforms into a golden masterpiece. Rise early or linger after dinner to capture these magical moments when the light bathes castles, vineyards, and quaint villages in a warm glow.
- **Play with Perspective:** Don't just stand and shoot! Climb to a hilltop for panoramic vistas, get down low for dramatic angles, or experiment with reflections in the water. A fresh perspective can transform an ordinary scene into something extraordinary.
- **Frame the Beauty:** Look for natural frames like arches, bridges, or overhanging branches to draw the eye into your composition. Incorporate leading lines like paths or riverbanks to guide the viewer through the scene.

Architectural Photography:

- **Focus on Details:** The Rhine boasts architectural gems, from grand cathedrals to charming half-timbered houses. Zoom in on intricate carvings, stained glass windows, or weathered stonework to reveal the stories etched in every detail.
- **Light and Shadow Play:** Use contrasts to create drama. Capture the interplay of sunlight and shadow on facades, or silhouette buildings against the fiery sunset. Remember, light is your brush, so use it creatively!
- **Unique Viewpoints**: Don't just shoot the front entrance! Explore narrow alleyways, peek through archways, or climb a tower for a bird's-eye view. These unexpected angles can reveal hidden beauty and add intrigue to your shots.

People and Culture Shots:

- **Capture Candid Moments:** Forget staged poses! Instead, focus on authentic expressions, laughter shared between friends, or a child chasing pigeons in a square. These genuine moments tell the story of the Rhine's vibrant culture.
- **Respect Local Customs:** Be mindful of privacy, especially in religious settings or small villages. Ask permission before photographing individuals, and always be respectful of their traditions.
- **Embrace the Quirky:** Don't shy away from the unusual! Capture colorful street performers, traditional costumes at a festival, or a local market overflowing with fresh produce. These details add character and charm to your photos.

Bonus Tips:

- **Pack the right gear:** A wide-angle lens is ideal for landscapes, while a zoom lens lets you capture distant details. Don't forget a sturdy tripod for low-light shots and a polarizing filter to reduce glare on water.
- **Be weather-ready:** Rain showers can add an atmospheric touch, but

protect your camera with a rain cover.

- **Edit with care:** Enhance your photos subtly, without overdoing it. Play with colors, sharpen details, and crop if needed, but remember to preserve the natural beauty of the Rhine.

Chapter 10: Practical Tips and Resources

Prepare for your Rhine River adventure with indispensable Practical Tips and Resources. Master essential language basics, manage currency and finances seamlessly, and leverage useful apps and gadgets for a smooth journey. Stay informed with safety guidelines, emergency info, and easy access to cruise line contacts and websites, ensuring a worry-free exploration.

Language Basics for River Cruise Destinations

Mastering basic language essentials enhances your Rhine River voyage. Learn common phrases in German, French, and Dutch, prevalent along the river's course. Embrace greetings, dining terms, and navigation phrases, fostering delightful interactions and cultural immersion, ensuring a seamless and enriching experience in these diverse river cruise destinations.

Greetings and Pleasantries:

- Guten Tag: Good day (formal)
- Hallo: Hello (informal)
- Auf Wiedersehen: Goodbye
- Bitte: Please
- Danke: Thank you
- Entschuldigung: Excuse me
- Ja: Yes

- Nein: No
- Prost: Cheers! (when raising a glass)

Essential Navigation:

- Wo ist ...? Where is ...? (e.g., die Toilette - the restroom)
- Wie komme ich zu ...? How do I get to ...? (e.g., dem Bahnhof - the train station)
- Kann ich bitte die Rechnung? Can I have the bill, please?
- Könnten Sie das bitte wiederholen? Could you please repeat that?

Dining Delights:

- Ich hätte gerne ... I would like ... (e.g., ein Glas Wein - a glass of wine)
- Können Sie mir ... empfehlen? Can you recommend ...? (e.g., ein gutes Restaurant - a good restaurant)
- Ohne ... bitte: Without ... please (e.g., Zucker - sugar)
- Ist das vegetarisch? Is this vegetarian?

Shopping Spree:

- Wie viel kostet das? How much does this cost?
- Kann ich das bitte anprobieren? Can I try this on, please?
- Nehmen Sie Karten? Do you accept cards?

Bonus Gems:

- Vielen Dank! Thank you very much!
- Es tut mir leid. I'm sorry.
- Zum Wohl! Cheers to your health!
- Alles Gute! All the best

Remember:

- A smile and a friendly attitude go a long way, even if your German is rusty.
- Don't be afraid to point and gesture; locals will appreciate your effort.
- Many Germans speak English, particularly in tourist areas, so don't hesitate to ask for help.
- Download a translation app for those tricky situations.

Learning basic numbers, days of the week, and common food items will further enhance your experience. Consider downloading a simple German phrasebook or enrolling in a beginner's course before your trip.

Pro Tip: Practice your German greetings and pleasantries with your cruise staff, fellow passengers, or even local shopkeepers. The more you engage, the more confident and comfortable you'll feel.

Currency and Money Matters

Understanding currency and money matters is crucial for a seamless Rhine River vacation. Navigate currency exchange and ATM accessibility along the route. Embrace smart budgeting tips and credit card acceptance to ensure smooth transactions, enabling you to focus on the scenic wonders and cultural treasures lining the picturesque Rhine.

The Euro Reigns Supreme:

The Rhine River winds through several countries, but one currency reigns supreme: the Euro (€). Familiarize yourself with its denominations (coins: €1, €2, €5, €10, €20, €50; notes: €5, €10, €20, €50, €100, €200) and practice basic counting.

Cash or Card? A Balancing Act:

While credit and debit cards are widely accepted, carrying some euros in cash is always wise. Smaller towns, quaint markets, and unexpected gratuities might not be card friendly. Aim for a mix, perhaps €200-€300 in cash for daily expenses and rely on cards for larger purchases and restaurant bills.

ATM Access:

ATMs are readily available in major towns and cities along the river. However, be mindful of potential foreign transaction fees levied by your bank. Consider informing your bank of your travel plans to avoid unpleasant surprises.

Tipping Etiquette:

Tipping in Germany is generally more relaxed than in some countries. Restaurants typically include a service charge in the bill, so rounding up slightly is enough. For taxis or exceptional service, a small tip (around €1-€2) is appreciated.

Budgeting for Bliss:

Plan your spending wisely. Factor in cruise fare, excursions, meals not included in the package, souvenirs, and gratuities. Research average prices for meals and activities to set realistic expectations. Consider pre-purchasing tickets for popular attractions to save money and avoid queues.

Hidden Costs to Avoid:

Beware of hidden fees! Currency exchange booths often offer unfavorable rates. Stick to ATMs or your bank for currency conversion. Some cruise lines might have onboard exchange services, but their rates might be less competitive.

Staying Connected:

Inform your mobile provider about your travel plans to avoid roaming charges. Alternatively, purchase a local SIM card upon arrival for affordable data and calls. Wi-Fi is generally available on board cruises and in many hotels and restaurants.

Tax-Free Shopping:

Non-EU residents can claim VAT refunds on purchases exceeding €25 in a single shop. Look for the "Tax Free Shopping" logo and keep your receipts. Upon departure, get your forms stamped at customs and claim your refund at the airport.

Embrace the Local Currency:

Learning a few basic German phrases related to money can go a long way. "Bitte" (please), "Danke" (thank you), and "Wie viel kostet das?" (How much does it cost?) will help you navigate everyday transactions with confidence.

Remember:

- Carry a mix of cash and cards.
- Inform your bank about your travel plans.
- Budget realistically for your expenses.
- Be mindful of hidden fees.
- Consider tax-free shopping opportunities.
- Learn some basic German phrases

With this guide as your compass, navigating the currency waters on your Rhine River Cruise will be a breeze.

Useful Apps and Gadgets

Useful apps and gadgets to enhance your Rhine River adventure. These apps help you with anything from navigation to translation. Waterproof cases and portable chargers, for example, ensure uninterrupted exploration. Enhance your journey along this historic canal with technology that simplifies and enriches your journey.

1. Essential Navigation:

- **DB Navigator App:** Your German train BFF. Plan your pre- and post-cruise journeys with ease, real-time updates, and offline ticket options. Download: https://www.bahn.de/service/mobile/db-navigator
- **Google Maps:** A universal friend, especially with offline maps downloaded. Plot your course, find hidden gems, and navigate charming alleyways with confidence. Download: https://play.google.com/store/apps/details?id=com.google.android.apps.maps&hl=en&gl=US
- **Citymapper App:** Your urban ally for navigating bustling cities like Cologne and Mainz. Public transport options, walking times, and live updates make getting around a breeze. Download: https://citymapper.com/?lang=en

2. Language Savvy:

- **Duolingo App:** Brush up on your German before you embark. Interactive lessons and gamified learning make language acquisition fun and effective. Download: https://www.duolingo.com/
- **Google Translate App:** Your real-time interpreter for menus, signs, and impromptu conversations. Point your camera, listen to translations, and conquer language barriers with ease. Download: https://translate.google.com/

3. Foodie Finds:

- **TripAdvisor App:** Your restaurant compass. Find Michelin-starred gems, local favorites, and hidden gems with user reviews, photos, and menus at your fingertips. Download: https://www.tripadvisor.com/
- **The Fork App:** Reservations made easy. Secure tables at popular restau-

rants, discover hidden treasures, and enjoy exclusive deals through the app. Download: https://www.thefork.com/

- **HappyCow App:** Vegan and vegetarian globetrotters rejoice! Find plant-based options near you, read reviews, and plan your delicious itinerary without the hassle. Download: https://www.happycow.net/

4. Handy Gadgets:

- **Portable Power Bank:** Never let a dead phone dim your foodie adventures. Keep your navigation apps and translation tools charged up with a reliable power bank.
- **Reusable Water Bottle:** Reusable water bottles are an environmentally responsible way to stay hydrated. Fill up taps or fountains and avoid plastic waste.
- **Headphones and Noise-Cancelling Earbuds:** Immerse yourself in local music, podcasts, or audiobooks while enjoying the scenic Rhine views. Noise-cancelling options help you tune out the world and savor the experience.

Bonus Tip: Download the cruise line's app! Access daily schedules, menus, shore excursions, and onboard activities, all at your fingertips.

Safety Guidelines and Emergency Information

Prioritize safety along your Rhine River journey with essential guidelines and emergency information. Familiarize yourself with safety protocols, emergency contacts, and health tips. Ensure a worry-free exploration by staying informed and prepared, safeguarding your memorable experience along this picturesque and historic waterway.

Know Your Ship:

- Familiarize yourself with the ship's layout, emergency exits, and muster stations. Participate in the mandatory safety drill – it's not just a formality, it's your lifeline in an unforeseen situation.

- Locate your lifejacket and ensure it's easily accessible.
- Understand the ship's whistle signals and protocols for emergencies.

Staying Afloat:

- Be mindful of railings and edges, especially on open decks, particularly when the ship is in motion.
- Wear appropriate footwear with good grip to navigate slippery decks, especially in wet weather.
- Remember, alcohol and water don't mix well. Be responsible with your consumption and avoid swimming while intoxicated.

Health and Hygiene:

- Pack essential medications and any prescription drugs you require.
- Carry over-the-counter relief for common ailments like headaches, stomach upsets, and allergies.
- Wash your hands frequently, especially before meals and after using public restrooms.
- If you experience any health concerns, don't hesitate to inform the onboard medical staff.

Staying Connected:

- Familiarize yourself with the ship's communication protocols in case of an emergency.
- Purchase a local SIM card or activate international roaming on your phone to stay connected on land.
- Download offline maps and essential phone numbers as internet access might be limited in certain areas.

Emergency Preparedness:

- Pack a small emergency kit with essentials like a flashlight, first-aid supplies, and bottled water.
- Keep copies of your travel documents, passport, and travel insurance readily accessible.
- Register with your embassy or consulate upon arrival in Germany for enhanced assistance in case of emergencies.

Additional Resources:

- European Emergency Number: 112
- German Federal Police: https://www.bundespolizei.de/
- Travel Advice for Germany: https://www.gov.uk/foreign-travel-advice/germany

Cruise Line Contacts and Websites

Access essential information for your Rhine River adventure with comprehensive cruise line contacts and websites. From renowned river cruise companies to niche operators, gather vital details and booking information. Explore their websites for itineraries, amenities, and embarkation details, ensuring a seamless and informed cruise experience along this scenic route.

Luxury Liners for the Discerning Traveler

Viking River Cruises: Renowned for their sleek Scandinavian design and intimate atmosphere, Viking boasts a fleet of modern ships like the Viking Star and Viking Vidar. Expect spacious cabins, attentive service, and curated shore excursions that delve into the region's history and culture.

- **Website:** https://www.vikingrivercruises.com/
- **Contact:** 1-800-300-9300

Scenic Cruises: If panoramic views are your priority, Scenic's innovative "Space Ships" like the Scenic Eclipse and Scenic Jewel are your answer. Floor-to-ceiling windows in every stateroom and public space, coupled with innovative "Dining by Design" options, promise an unparalleled connection to the Rhine's breathtaking landscapes.

- **Website:** https://www.scenic.com.au/
- **Contact:** 1-888-754-0500

Mid-Range Gems for Value Seekers

Uniworld Boutique River Cruises: Offering a blend of comfort and elegance, Uniworld's fleet like the River Countess and River Aria cater to a broad range of travelers. Expect regionally-inspired cuisine, themed voyages like "Christmas Markets on the Rhine" and "Castles of the Rhine," and engaging onboard activities.

- **Website:** https://www.uniworld.com/
- **Contact:** 1-800-738-6455

Tauck: Focused on immersive cultural experiences, Tauck's Rhine River program utilizes smaller ships like the MS Inspire and MS Grace. Intimate onboard settings, knowledgeable guides, and curated excursions that go beyond the usual tourist traps ensure a deeper understanding of the region's rich history and vibrant culture.

- **Website:** https://www.tauck.com/
- **Contact:** 1-800-455-2096

Family-Friendly Adventures

Avalon Waterways: Family-friendly amenities like dedicated kids' clubs, game rooms, and even waterslides on ships like the Avalon Impression and

Avalon Passion make Avalon a top choice for families. Expect engaging activities, shore excursions tailored for all ages, and a relaxed atmosphere onboard.

- **Website:** https://www.avalonwaterways.com/
- **Contact:** 1-800-256-6800

Emerald Waterways: Offering spacious cabins with family-friendly layouts and connecting doors, Emerald's ships like the Emerald Sky and Emerald Star cater to multi-generational travel. Expect interactive entertainment, engaging activities for kids, and shore excursions designed to appeal to the whole family.

- **Website:** https://www.emeraldcruises.com/
- **Contact:** 1-855-538-4758

Conclusion

As your Rhine River cruise glides towards its final port, watch the majestic castles blur into the horizon, their spires whispering tales of bygone eras. Let the rhythm of the river linger in your memory, a gentle counterpoint to the boisterous laughter and heartfelt conversations shared onboard.

But before you disembark, remember your voice matters! We'd love to hear your thoughts on your journey. Did the quaint villages charm you? Did the vineyards tantalize your taste buds? Did the historical sites ignite your imagination? Your feedback helps us refine our cruises, ensuring future travelers experience the magic of the Rhine anew.

So, as you bid farewell to the Rhine, know that its magic, like the whispers of the Lorelei, will forever captivate your soul. Auf Wiedersehen und gute Reise! (Goodbye and good travels!)